THE

PUBLICATIONS
OF THE
SURTEES SOCIETY

VOL. CLXXX

THE

PUBLICATIONS

OF THE

SURTEES SOCIETY

ESTABLISHED IN THE YEAR
M.DCCC.XXXIV

VOL. CLXXX

FOR THE YEAR MCMLXV

At a COUNCIL MEETING of the SURTEES SOCIETY, held in Durham Castle on June 6th 1968, Mr. C. R. Hudleston in the Chair, it was ORDERED—

"That Dr. A. M. C. Forster's edition of The Disbursements Book of Sir Thomas Haggerston should be printed as a volume of the Society's publications."

W. A. L. Seaman,
Secretary.

SELECTIONS FROM

THE
DISBURSEMENTS BOOK
(1691-1709)

of Sir Thomas Haggerston, Bart.

Printed by permission of Sir
Carnaby Haggerston, Bart.

EDITED BY

ANN M. C. FORSTER

PRINTED FOR THE SOCIETY BY
NORTHUMBERLAND PRESS LIMITED
GATESHEAD
1969

INTRODUCTION

The book from which these entries are taken is a large volume, with disbursements at one end and receipts at the other. The whole work is in one handwriting, that of Sir Thomas Haggerston, second baronet of Haggerston, a clear, bold hand, only towards the end growing feeble and straggling.

Entries give the date, the person to whom the money was paid, the nature of the transaction, the agent who made the actual payment, and the sum in figures. There is much repetition of items, and therefore selections only are given here.

Sir Thomas Haggerston was the eldest surviving son of Sir Thomas Haggerston, the first baronet and his wife Alice, daughter of Henry Banaster of the Bank, Lancashire. The father had fought in the service of King Charles I during the Civil War, holding a commission as colonel or Harquebussiers. He suffered much for his loyalty. His estates were seized and sold, and had to be bought back through the agency of John Brownell and Gilbert Crouch at a cost of something approaching £3,000 (S.S.CXI, 221).

His son, the second baronet, was born c. 1627-8, and held a commission as colonel of a regiment of Foot under the King. He was present with his father at the Muster of Gentlemen at Bockenfield on 29 January, 1660-1 (N.C.H.N. VII, 360 f.n.). In 1667 he was commissioned senior captain in the regiment of Foot raised by Lord Ogle, and was holding the same rank in 1673.

On 30 June, 1668, the estate being still burdened with debt, father and son entered into an agreement whereby Thomas junior, in consideration of an annuity of £50 and provision for the upkeep of Sir Thomas and his family at Haggerston, was to take over the estate and pay the debts. In this he seems to have been eminently successful. By the year 1691, when this book opens, he had begun to buy land, and as these accounts show, he was to purchase more in the years to come.

He married twice. His first wife was Margaret daughter of Sir

vii

Francis Howard of Corby, Cumberland, the mother of all his children. She died in 1673. His second was Jane, daughter and sole heiress of Sir William Carnaby of Farnham, Northumberland. He succeeded to the title on the death of his father in 1673-4.

Sir Thomas was Lieutenant-Governor of Berwick in 1688 when, with great jubilation, the town celebrated the birth of a son to the queen of King James II, and he and his lady entertained lavishly in honour of the occasion; but only a few weeks later he was attempting to raise a regiment to repel "this intended Invasion from Holland", with the result that, the following year, he found himself in custody. "Sir Thomas's zeal to the Catholic Cause is so well known, I need give no character of him," wrote the officer who had apprehended him. (*London Gazette*, 18-21 June, 9-12 July, 8-11 October, 1688; S.P. Dom. William & Mary, 1/73).

By 1691 however, the affair had blown over and he was back at Haggerston, living the quiet, ordered life of a country gentleman. Turning over these pages is like looking at a series of pictures which show that life in detail. We see the house with its stone-flagged hall, the hangings in the drawing-room, the closets and their painted wainscotting, the sash-window newly installed and the smoky chimneys. We note the number of domestics: six men servants, including three liveried, five or six maids, besides outdoor workers and casual labour; not a large staff considering all the work to be done—the house was almost self-supporting. Bread is never mentioned (except once for a funeral), cakes rarely; but we read of corn and wheat, and mills for grinding it. The further processes, up to the time the bread came to the table, would be carried on in the bake-house and stillroom. We note the purchase of milk-cows and the wages paid to the dairy-maid; all the produce of those cows would be the result of her handiwork. Butter indeed was bought in bulk, but only "to mend the hoggs", or "to grease the wains". There were payments to the ewe-milkers, who would lay the foundations for cheese; and indeed "my wife's cheeses" were exported as far as Stella. Once Sir Thomas indulged in "2 chesher cheeses" at a cost of 10s. 3d.

A frequent entry is "a veal calf for the house" bought of one of the tenants, in order to free the cow's milk for human consumption; and on the receipts end of the book (not here reproduced) there are entries of money received from the sale of hides and sheepskins, indicating that the beef and mutton had been used for the table. Bacon may be deduced from the employment of a "swine-boy", and entries concerning sows.

Fish was bought in quantity for Lent, cod, ling, sprats and herring, fresh and dried, and shell-fish, lobsters, oysters and cockles. Sir Thomas owned a coble and retained four fishermen to work it. Geese and ducks are mentioned, pigeons occasionally, and rabbits. There was fresh fruit in season, cherries and strawberries, apples and pears, and sometimes oranges. Sugar and spices were got from Berwick, or formed part of the grocery order placed once or twice yearly with Mr. Francis Brandling, merchant of New-castle. Possibly this order would include luxuries such as tea, coffee and chocolate, but they are nowhere mentioned.

Ale was home-brewed: there are payments for mending the brewing copper, for pulling heather to dry the malt, and for sifting it when dried. Brandy, sack and claret were purchased by the quart or the hogshead. The birth of an heir (February, 1697-8) was celebrated by a tremendous jorum compounded of brandy, wine, dried fruits and spices. "Rowle (rolled?) chawing tobacco" at 2s. the pound (3s. in Durham) was a luxury which Sir Thomas allowed himself.

Lighting would be entirely by candles, made at home, of beeswax bought in bulk, for the guest-rooms, and tallow doubtless for the kitchen. Heating was by coal, and there are payments made for leading it.

There are many entries concerning clothing, payments for spinning, weaving and bleaching and sometimes for dyeing cloth, but the more delicate materials, silk, cambric and muslin, were bought by the yard. Sometimes the cost of a suit or waistcoat is recorded, but often only the cost of making it. There is mention of cravats—a costly item—and of bone lace for ruffles. "My gold fringed black waistcoat and coat" and "my waistcoat of cloth of gold" indicate a gentleman of quality and perhaps necessitated the "muslin for my apron" which Sir Thomas enters on one occasion. There are payments for the making and repairing of wigs—long wigs, and bob wigs for riding—and for "sweet hair powder" bought of the "gingerbread man". Soap was got in bulk at 4s. a stone; "soap balls for shaving", as also razors. There is little to indicate toilet accessories for ladies. "Hungary water" was possibly a perfume, and the "red powder" prepared for Lady Haggerston may have been something in the nature of a cosmetic. Was it perhaps designed to disguise the anaemia caused by frequent blood-letting?

Sir Thomas's rent-roll in 1691 shows him to have had an income from rents and interest on loans, of roughly £1,200 a year. Some rents were paid by instalments, or made up in part payment by service or produce. He also farmed on a considerable scale. His sheep-count in 1696 was 58 score, in 1697 73 score, in 1702 67 score and in 1703 65½ score. Besides livestock, his receipts show sales of wool (12s. a stone), and of wheat, oats, barley, rye, peas and beans. Prices vary, but in 1696 they are given as being: wheat, 23s. a bole (a variable quantity, but usually 6 bushels), oats 12s. and peas 21s. a bole.

Wages were paid once or twice yearly, at Whitsuntide and Martinmas. Compared with present day standards they seem extraordinarily meagre, even allowing for differences in the value of money. The ordinary wage for a working man was 1s. a day. A mason got 1s. 6d. a day, as also a plasterer, or was paid by the piece. Casual harvest workers, "stranger mowers" received for the season's work, 1s. each; "half hinds" 5s. for the half year. Women were paid even less: for spinning, 8d. a week, for clipping sheep 6d. a day, no hours specified in either case. The ewe-milkers got about 4d. a week.

Domestic servants, of course, had their keep and perquisites in addition to wages. The coachman and senior men servants got £5 a year, the postillion £2 10s., the butler and head cook £3; the rest, £1 to £2 yearly. Nevertheless, some had money saved and invested with the master, who paid them interest at the normal rate of 6%. Besides these there was the housekeeper, "Cousin Fleetwood Butler", presumably a relative of the Margaret Butler who had been Sir Thomas's paternal grandmother. She controlled the household, paid the staff and many of the bills, and was an esteemed friend of the family, figuring in the wills of both Sir Thomas and Lady Haggerston.

About once a week Cousin Fleetwood Butler was given 5s. "for the use of the poor"; and frequently sums varying from 2s. 6d. to £1 were allotted to some individual "in charity". The term carried no stigma; it probably meant little more than "as a gift" as opposed to "for service rendered". Several of the recipients appear to have been ex-army officers, fallen on evil days; or tenants on the occasion of a wedding or the birth of a child.

Sir Thomas's own family consisted of sons. Thomas, the eldest, was already dead, killed in Ireland in 1690, fighting for King James II. He left two sons, Thomas and Francis. Thomas, named in his grandfather's will in 1695, was presumably dead in 1702, when Francis, who had entered the Benedictine Order, signed a deed by which, in consideration of an annuity of £50, he released all claims to the estate in favour of his uncle, William Haggerston.

This William, the second son, married, in 1695, Anne daughter of Sir Philip Constable of Everingham, Yorks. About 1702 they moved into the Haggerston house in Berwick. This had been badly damaged by fire in 1687, and entries extending over several years indicate repair work being done. William, as these accounts show, predeceased his father, dying in 1708.

The third and fourth sons, Henry and John, were both priests and members of the Society of Jesus. Henry appears to have been living throughout the period of these accounts at Haggerston. He probably filled the office of chaplain there. John, frequently at home, may be traced spending periods at Cartington, where Lady Charlton *née* Widdrington lived in her widowhood, and where there was a Catholic chapel; and at Widdrington.

Edward, the fifth son, married in 1693, Mary daughter of Gerard Salvin of Croxdale, county Durham. Under his marriage settlement he took Hazelrigg, for which his father paid him £120 p.a. rent, together with expenses arising out of the estate. In 1698 he purchased Ellingham—details of the conveyance appear in these accounts—and moved there, possibly after the rebuilding of the Hall, c. 1702. There are one or two indications that his brother John was then living with him. Sir Thomas allowed each of his married sons £60 a year.

Francis, the youngest son, had joined the Friars Minor of St. Francis and was ordained priest c. 1692. In 1694-5 he appears to have been supplying at Cartington. For the next four or five years he was in London, acting as Assistant to the Procurator, or Treasurer, of the Franciscans in England. After that his health broke down and he was sent home. There are entries of payments made by his father for doctors and physic for him. He seems to have been living with his brother at Berwick, for there he died, and was buried at Holy Island, 8 April, 1704.

Each of these priest sons had an allowance from his father of £20 p.a., and payments of these are here included in full, because the details give information, unobtainable elsewhere, of their whereabouts at the time the payment was made. When the money passed through the hands of Cousin Fleetwood Butler, we may reasonably conclude that the recipient was somewhere near at hand; when by a man servant, at some little distance, when by bill to London, either there or abroad.

Sir Thomas, as will have been gathered from the foregoing, was a Papist, and had been convicted of recusancy more than once in earlier days. The present period, however, was one of comparative toleration. Titus Oates had come and gone, and the unhappy days of the Jacobite risings were still in the future. This may be why it was possible for him, without fear of consequences, to include openly in his account book items such as "cambric to make an alb", "silver to make a pyx", and "eleven priests to pray for Sir Francis Tempest, deceased", items which would have been damning evidence of papistry only a few years earlier. He was, however, no bigot. Owning, as he did, tithes of Holy Island, he was responsible for the stipends of the curates in charge there and in the four dependent chapelries, Tweedmouth, Kyloe, Ancroft and Lowick, and these were paid regularly and correctly. He seems also to have claimed the right of presentation, and on one occasion made a handsome gift to his nominee when "balked by an act of Parliament". On another, he contributed a loan towards the burial expenses of the curate of Ancroft. There are entries of payments for repair of churches and for church wardens' expenses. Moreover, an item dated 13 October, 1692 is strongly suggestive of practical sympathy with the wife of the Presbyterian, Gabriel Semple.

A word may be said about sport. Except for references to "meat for the dogs", there is nothing which might suggest fox-hunting. Hawking was obviously popular from the entries of payments for hawks, and for their equipment and keep. One or two items suggest that Sir Thomas took an interest in horse-racing.

The first purchase of land mentioned in these accounts is that of Nuncloses in Holystone, bought from the Potts family of Farnham, in June, 1691. An entry in October of the same year marks the first negotiations for the acquisition of the Selby lands in Lowick and Kirknewton. These estates, after some litigation, had passed to Dorothy, daughter of George Selby, widow of Thomas Collingwood of Great Ryle and wife of Sir William van Colster, and her brother's widow Eleanor, daughter of Sir Francis Blake, now remarried to Charles Howard. (N.C.H.N. XI, 275 & XIV, 101). The van Colsters conveyed to Sir Thomas their property in Lowick in November, 1692, and Langleyford in December of the same year. The sale was completed in the June following. A mortgage of £1,100 on Branxton was taken over by Sir Thomas at the same time, and in March, 1694-5 Sir Mark Milbanke released all his claims on the Selby estates. In March, 1699-1700, the purchase of Branxton was completed. There appears to have been a charge on Lowick reserved to Sir Francis Blake, which was being paid in May, 1700. Monielaws was purchased in May, 1709.

There are references to the purchase of Ellingham by Edward Haggerston in 1698. Part of the purchase money was raised by a loan from Miss Mary Thornton of Witton Shields and her sister Helen, widow of Edward Widdrington of Blackheddon. The interest on this was paid by Sir Thomas Haggerston on his son's behalf.

Many entries refer to various forms of taxation, which, if not excessive in themselves, must by their very multiplicity, have been burdensome. Besides the demands of the Ecclesiastical Commissioners, there were the many forms of "sess"; house sess, bridge sess, window sess, cow sess. There was prison sess or gaol money, poor sess, rogue monie, land tax and militia horse money. These were all separately assessed for each portion of the estate and had various individual collectors.

The Lady Haggerston of this period was Sir Thomas's second wife, Jane Carnaby. Perhaps not too young herself, she seems to have coped admirably with an elderly husband and five grown-up sons. She had her circle of friends. Colonel William Strother of Fowberry had been a fellow officer of Sir Thomas in Lord Ogle's Regiment, and the Haggerstons maintained their friendship with him and his family, Mary Strother, married to Thomas Orde of Felkington, and Jane, the wife of William Carr of Eshott. There were card parties at their houses, and attendances, too, at confinements and christenings. There were visits to relatives at Biddleston, Callaly, Widdrington and Stella, and journeys to Berwick, Scotland, and occasionally to London.

But perhaps the greatest event of the year was the New Year dinner at Berrington, here recorded by the entry of tips to the servants and to the piper, and attended by every member of the family. "When we all dined there" is the entry year after year. The Claverings, by a relationship not easy to trace, were the "cousins" most intimate of all, connected by many ties of mutual esteem and service. "Cousin Jack Clavering" superintended the bringing of the coals from the pits on his estate; his sister Peggy fashioned Lady Haggerston's gowns. A similar feast seems to have been held at Haggerston at Christmas; and the piper, previously fitted with a new livery coat, was paid his fee "for piping in Christmas".

I am much obliged to Professor G. P. Jones, for notes on matters of finance, and Mr. W. Percy Hedley for genealogical findings.

A.M.C.F

THE DISBURSEMENT BOOK (1691-1709)
OF SIR THOMAS HAGGERSTON

(SELECTIONS)

1691.				£	s.	d.
Apr.	1.	To my wife for the use of the poore		0	5	0
	2.	To Bengy Greeve[1] for 1000 nailes and 2 pennyworth of pitch		0	8	2
	3.	To my wife for 23 yards of damask for napkings		1	10	8
	5.	To old Adam Smith[1] for £90 intrest due last 26 October		5	8	0
	8.	2 paire brass candellsticks for the alter by Robert Simmons		0	12	0
		To Matthew Sibbitt high Cunstable for 3 years muster and Trophee monie for all my estate		0	12	9
		For 6 quarts sack by Robert Simmons		0	11	0
		For 3 pound of Glew by Robert Simmons		0	2	0
		For Burgundy pitch by Robert Simmons		0	6	0
	10.	To the Berrington Smith for saddle horses shooeing and cleered with him to good fryday		0	11	8
	11.	To a poore prisoner to get him out of prison		0	7	0
		To my wife for a veale cawlfe for the house use		0	8	8
	18.	To Mr. Hyde in charity[2]		1	0	0
	20.	To Mrs. Ashley in charity		0	6	0
	21.	To my wife for shooes and slipers		0	5	4
	25.	To the Ord Brick maker for 3000 bricks by Anty Peacock		1	4	0

[1] Several Smiths of Scremerston are mentioned. Adam Smith was the father of the Margaret Smith who married William Brown of Bolton (SS. CXXXI, 17 f.n.) and grandfather of her daughter, wife of Benjamin Grieve. "Scremerston Willy Smith" (so called to distinguish him from Willy Smith of Haggerston) was often employed in engrossing legal documents.

[2] Item occurring about once a month.

Apr.	26.	To Watt Ashley[3] for a paire white Jersey stockens for my wife	0	3	0
May	5.	To Grace Grey dairy maide for Whittsonday wage by cosen Fleetwood	1	0	0
	10.	To Cudy Reed for Wine att Belford for my wife	0	9	8
	11.	For 2 blew chamber potts 1.8d. 2 white basons 2.2d. burgundy pitch 8d. In all	0	4	6
	12.	To my cosen Mary Haggerston[4]	0	5	0
		For 3 livery Hatts for Simmons, Maine and Steale	0	9	6
	12.	To the shepard of Lowlin for a little leane cowe by Willy Smith	0	10	0
	15.	To Robert Simmons for last half years wage due 25 March last	3	0	0
		To Tom Wilson for makeing and some part triming of 3 Liveres and wastcoates	1	6	4
	16.	To Tom Bell for a Cowe to feed by Willy Smith	1	15	0
		To Usy Beard for a cowe to feed by Willy Smith	1	6	0
		For 12 quarts Brandy to Mr. Albert Hodgson[5] by Robert Kellett	1	0	0
		A caske to putt the Brandy in	0	1	2
		To Robert Kellett for charges of bringing the wine and brandy from Neucastle	0	3	3
	18.	To widdow Purdy for a veale cawlfe for the house[6]	0	6	0
	19.	Lent Mr. John luck of Berwick £20 which he is to pay by bond and Judgment of next november after martinmas coming: it is payd X X X	20	12	0

[3] Walter Ashley (Astley) as a papist registered estate at Berwick in 1717 (SS. CXXXI, 126, 128). He was Sir Thomas's wig-maker. A William Ashley occurs in a list of Papists of Berwick, 1680 (H.M.C. Report No. 17, House of Lords 1678-88, C.15).

[4] Not identified; first of many such entries.

[5] Second son of John Hodgson of Jesmond and Anne his wife; admitted freeman of Newcastle, 1678 (Register Freemen 17 c. p. 95); mar. in 1668 Elizabeth Fenwick, widow; living in St. John's par. Newcastle, 1705 (Return of Papists 1705, House of Lords).

[6] A frequent item.

			£	s	d
May	21.	To my wife for 2 shifts to cosen Ann Howard	0	7	0
	21.	To Watt Ashley for a paire of stockens for cosen Fleetwood	0	3	6
	23.	To the farmer of Fleeup for a Galloway for sonn Hary	3	5	0
	24.	To Cudy Read for a years intrest of £60 due 25 last March '91	3	12	0
	27.	To William Archbould[7] for charges in sueing Boalum bond	4	19	10
		To William Archbould for charges in sueing the pottes bond	2	13	3
	31.	To Cudy Read for lime kill coales for Fenwick from Kyloe 56 scoare 12 bols	9	8	0
		To Cudy Read for the 12 halfe hynds wage of Fenwick and Buckton	3	0	0
		To the 9 Haggerston halfe hynds wage by Willy Smith	2	5	0
		To Lowery Atty for this halfe years wage by Willy Smith	1	5	0
		To Mathew swineboy for this halfe years wage by Willy Smith	0	10	0
		To Isabell Byars for wage now due by cosen Fleetwood	1	0	0
		To Mary Ivison for a part of wage by cosen Fleetwood	0	15	0
June	1.	To Willy Steall for a years wage due yesterday	4	0	0
		To Jenny Fenwick for halfe a years wage due yesterday by cosen Fleetwood	1	7	6
	1.	To Cudy Read for 27 wedders att Weetwood faire	8	7	2
	3.	To the 2 Potts to compleat the £700 for nunland closes purchase[8] by nephew Selby	38	7	8
		To young Wilson tayler for makeing 2 paire of britches with silck and thread	0	6	5

---

[7] Of Cawledge Park, Alnwick (N.C.H.N. VII, 373).
[8] See Introduction, p. xii.

		To my wife for wood vessells at Wooller faire	0	7	7
June	4.	To the 2 Potts for the purchase of nun-closes[8]	700	0	0
		To Joseph Pattyson cleering all smith worke to this day	2	0	0
		To Dicky Daye for limestones breaking by Willy Smith	0	2	4
	7.	To sonn Will Haggerston for this paste years pention by cosen Fleetwood	30	0	0
		To sonn Ned for this years paste pention[9] by cosen Fleetwood	30	0	0
		To sonn Hary for this paste years pention by cosen Fleetwood	10	0	0
		To sonn Jacky for this paste years pention[10] by cosen Fleetwood	10	0	0
	8.	To mace James Douglas in charity	0	6	0
	10.	To Joseph Dickyson for 2 chesher cheeses by Robert Simmons	0	10	3
		To the Cooper for this halfe years wage by cosen Fleetwood	0	11	6
		To widdow Shell for £100 intrest Tho not due till the 20 July next by James Lee	3	0	0
		To Isabell Byars weding for my wife and selfe by cosen Fleetwood	0	12	0
	10.	To Dolly Carnaby to spend at Isabell's weding	0	1	6
	16.	To my wife at Mrs. Ashley's upsitting by cosen Fleetwood	0	5	0
		To James Nealson for 84 yards of fine muriseland cloath, in 4 webbs	7	14	0
	17.	For all my estate in Bishopbrigg for 2 bridges duble sess att 10 in the pound	4	13	10
		To my cosen Claverings and my owne sheep sheerers	0	7	0
		To Marke Potts[11] payd by nephew Charles			

---

[9] See Introduction, p. xi.
[10] See Introduction, p. xi.
[11] The vendor of Nuncloses; the money was to be paid by Charles Selby, who rented the Carnaby lands in Farnham from Sir Thomas.

		Selby of my wifes highlands Rents and being allowed him in accounts	160	0	0
June	18.	To Robert Simmons for a veale cawlfe for the house use	0	10	0
		To Mr. Countan for wood for a sash window by Robert Simmons	0	11	0
		To Bengy Griefe for 1000 3d tacketts by Robert Simmons	0	2	6
	20.	To my wife for blanketting	0	6	8
		To Will Ollifant and his sonn for plaistering the buttry entery my closet and little roome	0	15	0
	21.	To Cudy Read for sheep sheering '91	0	15	6
	24.	To Cudy Read for 12 score bols Kyloe coales for lime burning for Fenwick and Buckton	2	0	0
	25.	To James Nealson for 21 yards fine muerissland Lining cloath	2	5	6
July	1.	My charges to Bidleston[12] the 29 June '91	2	4	8
	2.	To Mr. Thomas Bowelby of Darneton sadlar for 6 bridles with snafels and with six paire stirup leathers	0	17	4
	4.	To James Nealson by my wife for 63 yeards of Dyper for napkins	2	7	3
	6.	To caridge of wheat to Anwick and Wool' toule and charges by Cudy Read	0	3	0
		To Cudy Read for 2 sacks of haire att Anwick for 4 paire little sizer [sic] and 200 needles	0	2	4
		To the Gosewick Gardiner by wife for bring a baskett of Cherryes	0	1	6
	9.	To George Rose for meate for the house use cleering all meate to this day	1	1	0
		To George Rose for 6 kyloes for feeding	9	0	0
	10.	For glew and 1 peece of cording for my sash window by Robert Simmons	0	1	7
		Young Robert Kellett charges to neucastle for soape and grossary	0	2	5

[12] Home of the Selbys, Charles Selby and his wife Elizabeth, *née* Gillibrand.

	To Mr. Edminson for 6 halfe pound of Rowle chaweing tobaco by Robert Simmons		0	6	0
	For second quarter sess for my house in Barwick		0	9	0
	My wife's charges att Ladye Morrisons in Scotland		0	3	6
	To my mad cosen Mary Haggerston		0	2	6
	To Squire Clavering of Callaly[13] for 2 paire wheels for Buckton by Cudy Read		3	0	0
July	15.	To Berrington malt man for makeing 18 kills of malt by Willy Smith	1	7	0
	15.	To Cudy Read for 3 dozen waine clouts 7s. 6d. for 5 paire waine roaps 2s. 8d. for 2 dozen halters and traces 2s. 8d. for a dogg skinn 6d. Cudy's and Will Smith's charges att Anwick faire and amongest my wifes Tennents in getting in rents: In all	0	19	8
		To Joseph Foster for glasing pluming and all maner of other work to this day	6	0	0
		To Sander Udney for makeing my closett sash window	1	4	0
	16.	To George Boory of Barwick one of the mayers sargants in charity	0	1	2
	17.	To Willy Smith for butter for to grease the wains	0	1	2
	24.	To seven stranger mowers att Haggerston by Willy Smith	0	7	0
	26.	To Cudy Read for 2 scyeths att Wooler	0	4	0
	30.	To John Winlow Island for 40 dryd killing £1 6s. od.; for 10 ling 10s. In all	1	16	0
		To James Blacklock for a maile leather monie bagg	0	4	0
Aug.	1.	To the weemen that sifted 18 kill of the malt of the kill	0	4	6
		To a spinner woman for 8 weeks spining for my wife	0	5	4

---

[13] Ralph Clavering (d.1692/3). Wheels from Callaly are mentioned more than once.

	To a pedlar for 3 paire of large sissers	0	0	9
Aug. 12.	To repaire sonn Ned's loss at Widdrington 15 ginnies and £3 in monie in all	19	10	0
13.	To Anty Peacock for finding Anwick maire foales melt	0	0	4
	For 13 Raysors for myselfe and sonns	0	14	1
14.	To Willy Smith for 4 sickells for the hynds	0	1	0
16.	To the 4 carryers of my wooll to Anwick by Cudy Read	0	4	0
	To carrage and toule and charges of 10 bols wheat to Anwick and Wooler	0	10	6
17.	To Berrington sheerers by Willy Smith for a days sheering	0	8	6
18.	To the mayer sargant of Barwick for bringing the neuse letter and Gazette	0	1	0
23.	To Goswick warner for 2 cuple Rabatts by Willy Smith	0	2	0
24.	To an old oxe bowe maker for 3 dozen oxe bowes by Willy Smith	0	7	0
27.	By my wife to her nurse in charity	2	0	0
28.	To my wife for Table cloathes napkings and course Ticking and 2 yards scotch cloath for cosen Mary Haggerston	4	6	2
31.	To Mr. John Douglas Neucastle Towen clark for Attorney fees cleering to this day	14	15	0
Sept. 7.	To sonn Will for a lame Gallowaye	3	0	0
14.	To nephew Charles Selby[14] allowed of rent for 20 steers	80	0	0
	To nephew Charles Selby allowed of rent for 8 steers had of Jeffery Younge of Farnham and 1 stirk all bought by Cudy Read	19	12	0
	To George Jemmyson of Battleshield haugh for 2 stirks by Cudy Read	2	6	0
	To Dandy Burns of Soureup for 10 steers	31	13	4
	To old Will Buddle for 11 stirks	13	4	0

[14] Second son of William Selby of Biddleston (d.1642) and Helen Haggerston, sister of Sir Thomas.

Sept. 15.	To Cudy Reads charges with toule of all these beasts bought att Harbottle faire	0 16 0
	To cosen Fleetwood for scotch cloath for a shaving cloath	0 4 0
19.	To James Nealson for a paire of brass weights and seals for my wife att St. Rinian faire[15] by cosen Fleetwood	2 6 8
	For course cloath bee waxes and some wood vessell for my wife's use and some boane lace	
	To Gordon shipmaster for bringing 1000 plaistering latts from Neucastle payd by Robert Simmons	0 6 0
	For an oxe stirk at St. Rinian faire by Cudy Read	1 10 0
22.	For 6 pound of bee waxe by cosen Fleetwood	0 5 0
	To Willy Smith for a years wage and washing due att Michaelmas coming	5 16 0
	To old Helen Kellett for 2 pookes for the granary use by Willy Smith	0 4 0
	For 2 further hather pulling for drying malt att Berrington	0 5 0
24.	To Igg Maine[16] for 6 pound of waxe	0 5 0
	To cosen Clavering of Berrington[17] for a fatt cowe	3 15 0
28.	To Mr. Medcalfe in charity	1 0 0
29.	To Mr. Arthur Edminson Barwick for 2 pound of tobaco by Robert Simmons	0 4 0
	For 4 pound of beeswax to cosen Fleetwood	0 3 4
30.	To James Stobs for iron for my closett by Robert Wilson Smith	2 2 11

[15] St. *Ninian*'s fair was held at Fenton annually in September, with a show of sheep, cattle and horses. (Mackenzie, *Northumberland*, I, 392.)

[16] The first of several of that name in the service of the Haggerston family. (See SS. CXXLIII, 74, 91.)

[17] John Clavering of Berrington was the son of William, younger brother of Ralph Clavering of Callaly (d.1682/3) and Barbara, daughter of Henry Lambton. John Clavering died unmarried in February, 1743/4. His brother William and sister Margaret also lived at Berrington.

To Robert Wilson Smith for all kinde of worke for the closett and old clock and bell	1	12	2
To cosen Jack Fenwick of Nunriding[18] in charity £1 and to Rayph Browen of Witton 5s.	1	5	0

Oct. 1. To Mr. Stephen Jackson mayre of Barwick for theire sixt part of Cheswick tyeth as by Lease for Michaelmas '91 Rent by Robert Simmons   9 0 0

To Mr. Bengy Greeve for gold in scotch monie   12 16 0

To Bengy Greeve for 2 bed cords for the bell   0 4 0

To Bengy Greeve for small nailes at severall times 6000   1 1 10

4. To Cudy Read for 2 bols seed Rye att Wooler with charges   1 2 6

7. To sonn Jacky for a white maire by cosen Fleetwood   3 0 0

10. To Mr. Robert Jackson of Stockton for 50 bols wooll measure for seed cleveland seed wheat   70 4 0

To Mr. Robert Jackson 112 lb. casell[19] soape for my wife   1 12 0

10. To William Carr for fraught of the wheat to Fenham   3 15 0

To the Custom office for a bill of unloading and the return of the Cockett[20]   0 4 6

Roger Maine's charges to Neucastle with the seed wheat monie for Mr. Jackson   0 9 6

16. To Mr. Wirge minister of Kirknewton for Dunsdall Tyeth at michellmass '91[21]   2 0 0

---

[18] A younger son, born after 1615 of George Fenwick, of Langshaws and Nunriding, and Barbara, daughter of Robert Mitford of Mitford, George Fenwick's mother was a Haggerston.

[19] i.e. Castile.

[20] A form of receipt.

[21] Dunsdale in "Selby's Forest" was conveyed by George Selby in 1673.

		Charges at Woller haugh head[22] with nephew Selby and Lady van Coulster[23]	0	4	0
Oct.	18.	To Cudy Read for layeing the hoggs	0	15	0
		To cosen Clavering of Berrington for 5 firkings of Butter for laying the hoggs	2	16	0
		For a banner and bannerett to Mr. Dowens by Jack Dixson	7	0	0
		Jack Dixsons charge in fetching them from London by land a horseback	3	11	11
	21.	To Nelly Hall for a present of six duck from the lady of Berrington to my wife	0	1	2
	22.	To young William Ollivant for plaistering the nursery	1	5	6
	22.	To the five Chappelrys for minister's stypends last Michellmass[24]	25	0	0
		The third quarter sess of Barwick house by Robert Simmons	0	9	0
	25.	To my cosen Mary Haggerston for a paire of shooes by Robert Simmons	0	2	0
	26.	To Cudy Read for 5 dozen glass bottles by Robert Simmons	0	12	8
		To my wife for 2 paire of sheetts bought of Mary Ivison	0	16	0
	27.	To the 2 Potts wives when they joyned with their husbands in passing the fine of Nuncloses	20	0	0
		To Cudy Read and Willy Smiths charges when the fine was past	0	13	2
	30.	To William Wilson of Hodesden for a younge bull	3	6	8
Nov.	5.	To Stuart the pedler for lace and Holland by my wife	2	6	10
	6.	To the Comisiṅy Court for the change of Churchwardens	0	4	7

[22] The remains of this famous old inn are still standing.

[23] See Introduction, p. xii.

[24] Holy Island, Tweedmouth, Ancroft, Kyloe and Lowick. Sir Thomas paid £20 p.a. to each out of tithes. Mr. Patrick Smith had been Curate of Tweedmouth since 1665; he also served Kyloe, and Ancroft after the death of Mr. John Wood in August, 1692. Mr. John Udney served Holy Island 1667-1695, and was then succeeded by Dr. James Cooper.

		To widdow Purdy of Brockmill for grind-ing malt from her	2	0	0
		To Widdow Purdy of Brockmill for 2 mens harvest wages	1	11	4
Nov.	9.	To Nelly Smith for pulling hadder for dry-ing malt and wyer for ringing swine	0	7	2
	11.	Wages: maids Mary Hall cook,	1	10	0
		Jenny Fenwick,	1	7	6
		Nelly Davy, Mary Morrison, Jenny Bro-wen, £1 each;	3	0	0
		Mathew the Butler	1	10	0
		Lowery Atthy	1	5	0
		Mathew Howattson swine boy	0	10	0
		To the Inhabitants of Haggerston of har-vest worke from martinmas '91 to mar-tinmas '91 [sic]	81	14	9
		Jemmy Hann for butchering from Martin-mass '90 to Martinmass '91	0	8	0
		William Bell for 30 yards cloath weaveing for my wife	0	7	6
	23.	To Robert Simmons for intrest of £50 but not due till next cristmas	3	0	0
		To Robert Simmons for halfe a years wage due michellmass last	2	10	0
		To Robert Simmons for his maides harvest wage '91	0	12	10
		To Dick Short Island for 70 codfish £2 9 0 and 10 ling 12s. In all	3	1	0
		To my 4 sonns Anueties halfe years now last Martinmass by cosen Fleetwood	80	0	0
	26.	To Mrs. Wilkyes midwife and nurse att her crissening[25] by my wife	0	5	0
Dec.	1.	To George Penny's weding and widdow Purdy's by Willy Smith	0	10	0
		To Tom Wilson tayler for makeing my winter coate by cosen Fleetwood	0	7	6
	1.	To Ralphe Sammon soldier [sic] for a Jack	1	10	0

[25] Elizabeth, sister of Francis Brandling, merchant of Newcastle and wife of John Wilky of Broomhouse. The child would be Catherine Wilky, baptized 26 November, 1691 (H.I. reg.).

Dec.	7.	To Mr. Busby for an old fawcon	2	10	0
	9.	To sonn Hary for Derrick Gardner's charges in coming from Leege	2	0	0
		To cosen Peggy Clavering for a silck mantua and petty coat for my wife with lyning fring making and other trimings needful	8	9	1
		To Peggy Clavering for fring and cotton thread	0	8	2
		To Tom Forster by order from the Deputie Leutns for my malicia horse for my wife's estate for the year 1691 by Willy Smith	8	0	0
		To cosen Fleetwood for 3 yards of small gold lace in Edminsons shop	0	1	9
	14.	To Willy Smiths charges when he went to get Robin Widdringtons[26] malicio monie [sic]	0	3	6
		To Tom Meudy miller for 3 days' moweing and a halfe	0	3	6
		To Hary Wattson wright for a years worke att Haggerston being 71 days	1	15	6
	22.	To Cudy Read by his grandchild Tom Smith for hewing wood in Fenwicke parke	8	3	10
		To a pedler for lace for a shift sleeves ruffells 2 yards	0	2	0
	24.	To Robert Simmons for my wife's blew cloath dyeing att Anwick with charges	0	14	0
		To Robert Simmons for fraught of grocery from Neucastle for my wife	0	3	0
		To the smith of Fenwick for 2000 flawes locks bolts and bands for a new barne	1	0	6
	30.	To Charles Robinson smith for shoeing for 2 ploughs and all other worke	5	1	2
	31.	To Roger Maine for a year's wage	5	0	0
		To Roger Maine for intrest of £50	3	0	0
		To Roger Maine for his maide harvest wage	0	13	4

[26] Possibly Robert Widdrington of Hawksley.

(*1691/2*)

Jan.	1.	In Neu years gifts by my wife and myselfe given	15 7 4
	8.	To the Berrington piper att severall times and servants when wee all dined	1 0 0
		To John Robison piper for piping in cristmas	0 6 0
		To 2 watches to sonn Hary and Jacky given by my wife	6 10 0
	10.	To Gallan the piper for a paire of dubble pypes and a paire of great	1 9 0
		To Mr. Bell marchant in Barwick for 24 yards clockstring by Robert Simmons	0 3 0
	14.	To Robert Cooke for brandy cleering all accounts to this day for brandy	6 1 4
		To an Anwick glover for 3 paire of gloves	0 5 0
	15.	To my wife a ginny sent to her nurse by her sonn Mr. Adamson	1 2 0
		To Willy Smith his charges getting Mr. Robert Widdrington's 6 years arears £12 due 29 Sept. '91 for his fift part of malicia horse joyned to mine	0 6 8
	22.	To sonn Ned for a black quilted sadle	1 2 0
	25.	To Willy Smith for draweing the writings betwixt the Lambs of Cheswick and me for conveing the Pryor of Glebe lands there to me	0 7 6
Feb.	2.	To cosen Fleetwood Butler for sallary this halfe year now due	4 0 0
	4.	To sonn Hary for stocking locking jumping and brithing the longe gunn	0 9 8
		To Mathew Byarley buttler for this halfe yeare wage	1 10 0
	10.	To sonn Francis[27] £100 for 5 years anuety; to Mr. Joseph Dickyson for takeing it in Scotch monie and for returning it to London 50s. In all	102 10 0
	15.	For my last quarter's sess for Barwick house	0 9 0

---

[27] See Introduction, p. xi.

		For the Towen years rent and 2 water cocks and pypes for Barwick house	0	4	6
Feb.	22.	To cosen Fleetwood Butler for a fringed handcoucher	0	2	0
	26.	To Willy Smith for butter to mend the hoggs	0	1	8
March	6.	To Mr. Robert Pringle for 39 quarts of clarett	2	12	0
	22.	To cosen Fleetwood for cockells of Endimion Scott 6 pecks	0	4	0

1692.

	25.	To Mrs. Ashley for knitting a paire of cotton stockens	0	2	6
	26.	To Moysess tayler for makeing Dolly Carnabys Cloaths	0	8	0
	28.	To Willy Smith to paye the Easter reckonings for Haggerston for '91	0	4	8
Apr.	12.	To the 5 Chappellryes for Lady day stypends to Mr. Smith and Mr. Udney	25	0	0
	18.	Spent among the poale [27a] commissioners	0	3	0
	19.	To the sowe gelder by Willy Smith	0	1	2
	25.	To Will Archbould to cleer Nunclose fine and all other fees to this day	9	18	0
May	6.	To Mr. Widdrington in charity by my wife	0	10	0
	7.	To Mr. Chattoe for 3 liveries and to young Wilson for makeing them	9	15	4
		To Mr. Chattoe for coate for waistcoate for myselfe and to young Wilson for makeing them	9	13	0
		To Mr. Chattoe for scarlett kattine [sic] £1 and 10 yards dimmetty 10s. In all	1	10	0
	14.	To my wife's nurse by her sonn Adamson vicker	0	11	0
	25.	To my 4 sonns for anneutys this Whittsonday '92 by cosen Fleetwood	8[0]	0	0

[27a] i.e. poll.
[28] The Priory land in Beal, settled on John, younger son of William Selby of Beal (d.1671) and conveyed by him to Sir Thomas Haggerston.

June	5.	To providing £1500 for Beall purchase[28] with a jorney to Neucastle	50	0	0
		To 2 more Jurneys to Neucastle about cosen Rayph Brandling's business[29]	5	0	0
		To cosen Hary Lambton[30] for 3 retaining fees at Neucastle	1	10	0
		To mr. Prouve for a vizard rideing maske	0	10	0
		To Mr. Prouve for mending 3 watches	0	8	0
	5.	For things for my wife at Neucastle in Easter weeke '92	3	0	0
July	14.	To the midwife and nurse att Cudy Reads sonns crissening	0	15	0
	22.	To sonn Will for pockett monie by cosen Fleetwood Butler	14	8	0
	24.	To Cudy Read for carrage of 1 shipload bigg and 2 of wheat to Fenham	1	14	6
	27.	To Michell Davisson of Langley ford for guiding me up to Chiviott	0	3	4
Aug.	7.	Lent Mrs. Wood to bury her minister husband with[31]	1	0	0
	9.	To Cudy Read for cockles in lent for the house use	0	16	0
Sept.	15.	For 20 young steers at Harbottle faire of Gabriel Hall nephew Charles Selby to pay for them out of arrears of rent	60	0	0
		To charity uses for F.T. by my order payd by nephew Charles Selby	11	0	0
		To nephew Charles Selby for 2 Fenwick millstones from Harbottle Craggs[32]			
	29.	To Tweedmouth brickmaker for 1000 bricks	0	8	0
Oct.	3.	To Mr. Hyde for a yallow paced gelding of Lowdians kynde	7	0	0

[29] Probably Ralph Brandling of Hoppen, though Francis Brandling his brother, frequently mentioned here, is never termed "cousin". Also living at this time were Ralph Brandling of White House, Alnwick, and Ralph Brandling of Felling.

[30] Son of Henry Lambton of Lambton Esq. & Mary Davison of Blakeston; brother of Mrs. Barbara Clavering of Berrington; Deputy Recorder for Newcastle in 1686. (Surtees, *Durham* II 175).

[31] Cf. n. 24.

[32] Millstones are still to be seen on this site.

	For 25 young steers summering at Langley ford by Cudy Read	3	2	6
Oct.	3.	In charity of Mr. Semple and setting her to Edenbrough[33]	1	15	0
		To Mr. Faire Barwick for one dram of Bontious pills	0	1	6
	4.	To Mrs. Thorold for my wife's use returned to London by Mr. Joseph Dickyson marchant	20	0	0
	10.	To Tom Smith for the postage of comission and lease for a yeare of Langlayford	0	2	0
	18.	To Mrs. Ashley for knitting a paire of cotton stockings	0	2	6
		To Elizabeth Singleton for one old fallen house in Barwick standing on the back of my garden next the back Gaite	2	0	0
	22.	To Robin Cooke for a hoggshead of wine	10	0	0
	25.	To my wife att Mary Smiths of Scremerston lying in	0	2	6
		To Mary Attichison's daughter's weding by Willy Smith att Barwick	0	10	0
	29.	To the carriers for bringing grossary from Neucastle	0	7	9
Nov.	1.	To Jemy Crawford's brother and Olliver Tompson's daughters weding	0	10	0
	23.	To William Ollivant for all work for plaistering the staire case 66 days work	5	0	0
		To William Browen for 24 days for hewing flaggs for the Hall	1	4	0
	23.	To John Scrowder for hewing flaggs for the Hall 8 days with his prentice	0	13	4
		To sonn Will for this halfe yeare's pention by cosen Fleetwood	33	10	0
		To sonn Ned for this halfe year's pention by cosen Fleetwood	30	0	0
		To sonn Hary for this halfe year's pention by cosen Fleetwood	10	0	0

---

[33] Almost certainly the wife of the Presbyterian divine, Gabriel Semple. (A.A. (3) IX, pp. 3 ff.)

	To sonn Jacky for this halfe year's pention by cosen Fleetwood	10	0	0
Nov. 28.	To John Robison pyper for pyping in harvest	0	5	0
	The charges of the Church wardens att Spittle	0	3	6
	Charges for aresting and entering Tom Sibbit action	0	0	8
	To Rayph Heath for 300 marble flaggs wining	2	13	2
	To the satcher for satching here and att Holly Island	0	9	0
29.	To Sir William van Colster for the present purchase and revertion of Lowick after the death of Mrs. Howard who was Mr. George Selby's of Twisell widdow £1000 and 20 ginnies to my Lady van Colster In all[34]	1022	0	0
Dec. 8.	To Sir William van Colster in part of Langley ford purchase with £300 before and £200 now, by Willy Smith and Roger Maine att Twisell payd £100 monie and by bill charged of Alderman Nicholas Fenwick of Newcastle in all[35]	700	0	0
12.	For charges mending the slate roofs of Barwick house	0	1	2
12.	To Mathew Lintell for fraught of goods to Barwick for the old chamber	0	18	4
20.	To Mrs. Thorold a £20 bill from Mr. Edward Nealson drawen upon Mr. Joseph and Mr. Jackson att 8 days sight for the use of my wife	20	0	0
24.	To young Wilson tayler Barwick for the pypers livery coate by cosen Fleetwood	1	3	0
28.	To Mr. Neugent in charity—20 marks [sic]	1	3	4

[34] See Introduction p. xiii.
[35] See Introduction p. xiii.

1692/3
Jan.   1.   To Hugh Magduggall for carrying a letter
             to Sir George Seaton by sonn Ned   0 6 0
        4.   For munth sess for Barwick house   0 18 0
       20.   My charges to see nephew Selby of his
             broaken legg at Bidellston   0 13 0
             To Sr. William and Lady van Colster each
             a ginny att the contract for Lowick pur-
             chase   2 4 0
       26.   Spent at Betty Simmons buriall of cosen
             Clavering and Fleetwood in Ancroft   0 4 0
Feb.   4.   To my wife for 460 red herren att the
             Island for the house use   0 10 3
       17.   To a Blankett man for a paire of fine blan-
             ketts   1 10 0
             To him for a paire of course blankets 6s.
             for coverletts 18s.   1 4 0
             To him for 2 callico quilts   2 10 0
       22.   To a blankett man for 2 ticks 2 boulsters
             att Barwick   1 7 6
             To cosen Fleetwood for a paire of brass
             sniffers and pann at Barwick   0 2 4
             To Lewis Alder in charity   0 1 2
       22.   To Jane Forster in charity by cosen Claver-
             ing   0 5 0
March 16. For 300 white herring for the house use att
             Cornewell   0 7 6
       23.   To cosen Fleetwood for my wife to Gose-
             wick midwife and nurse   0 4 8
             To Cudy Midford for drawing and en-
             grossing lease and release for Lowick   2 0 0
             To Cudy Midford 4 days rideing charge
             about the saile of Lowick   0 10 0

1693.
Apr. 10. Charges att meeting Cosen Salvine[36] att
             Bidleston   0 11 0

[36] Gerard Salvin of Croxdale; his daughter Mary and Edward Haggerston were married this year.

Apr.	18.	To the Island church sess for Milkhouse	0	5	0
	23.	To Lady van Colster att her and Sir William passing Lowick fine 20 ginnies	22	0	0
		My charges then to Cartington sarvants	0	12	0
	30.	To Mrs. Thorald for sonn Francis anuety due 25 March '93 by bill to London by Dickenson	20	0	0
May	6.	To Sir William van Colster lost of Sir Francis Tempest maire	4	10	0
	16.	To Mr. Smith and Mr. Udney for serveing the 5 chaples due 25 last March	50	0	0
	23.	Robert Simmons charges with the coach to Cartington	0	3	3
June	9.	To squire Ogle of Cawsey park[37] for 7 gauge of wheel spoakes	2	2	0
	18.	Sonns Hary and Jacky annuities	20	0	0
July	9.	Sonn Will . . . sonn Ned annuities	60	0	0
		To my wife in charity to her nurse in Durham	0	10	0
		To old Jack Fenwick att Lansheth[38] in charity	0	5	0
		For 6 spoons att Neucastle of Mr. Ramsey[39]	3	3	0
		For 6 forks att Neucastle of Mr. Ramsey	3	9	6
		For 6 trencher salts at Neucastle of Mr. Ramsey	3	3	8
		My charges to Stella about Sir Francis Tempest accounts takeing[40]	8	0	0
		To Mr. Ramsey for 2 gold haire rings given by my wife to my 2 neece Tempests	1	10	0
	19.	To the repaire of Island church by the Milkhouse	0	5	0
		To the repaire of Island church by Haggerston	1	1	6

[37] William Ogle of Cawsey park had married Elizabeth, 3rd daughter of Col. William Strother of Fowberry.

[38] Langshaws; the same person as the Jack Fenwick of Nunriding, previously mentioned. Cf. n. (18)

[39] For the family of Ramsay, goldsmiths of Newcastle, see AA (3), XI 100-103.

[40] Son of Sir Thomas Tempest of Stella (d.1691) and Alice daughter of William Hodgson of Hebburn and Margaret Haggerston sister of Sir Thomas died September 1698. The nieces were his sisters, Jane, later wife of William 4th, Lord Widdrington, and Iroth Tempest.

		To the repaire of Island church by Buckton	1	1	6
		To the repaire of Island church by Fenwick	1	1	6
July	22.	To my wife for cloath Mrs. Selby of Low-lin bought in Scotland	1	0	0
	26.	To cosen Jack Clavering of Berrington for a foale by my wife	1	0	0
	30.	To cleer Langleyford purchase in Jan. '92 to Sir William van Colster and lady	320	0	0
	30.	To Lord Midleton of Branxton morgage redeeming in 82 August the 8[41]	1100	0	0
		To Sr. William van Colster in part of Lowick purchace 710; to Mr. Burell & Lester payd by Edward Burdett[42] the first 300 April '93. the last £410 the 11 8br. '93. The remaining 300 is secured by bond for cleering so far Sr. Marke Milbanks moiety of morgage upon the whole estate[41]	710	0	0
Aug.	7.	My wifes charges att Lady Morrysons in Scotland	0	2	6
	9.	Allowed George Smith for the court dinner and charges in 93 out of fines	3	5	8
	13.	To Cudy Reed for the last shiploads of corne from Fenwick and Buckton carring	0	15	9
		To Cudy Reed for 36 days ditching att Hazellrigg att 6d the daye	0	18	0
	25.	To the Labourer that sarved Will Todd att slateing Barwick house	0	8	0
Sept.	8.	For 20 three year old stotts att Harbotle faire by Cudy Reed and Willy Smith	70	0	0
		For 5 three year old stotts att Harbotle faire by Cudy Reed and Willy Smith	13	6	8
		Att Tom Ashley's crissening	0	10	6
		Charges att meeting Mr. Salvin in Neucastle	8	0	0
Oct.	3.	To Mr. John Blithman for 12 Wooler bols of Cleevland seed by Anty Peacock	20	0	0

[41] See Introduction p. xiii.
[42] Son of Edward Burdett of Willimontswick; admitted to Grays Inn 1664.

	To 8 Berrington men and 4 of my own for bringing the seed wheat home	3	12	0
Oct.	10. To sonn Ned sent by his sarvant Jemmy Craford to outon	10	0	0
	11. To John Robinson for pyping in harvest	0	6	0
	19. To Mr. Fenwick for a boxe carrying from London	0	3	6
	22. To Andrew Morton for 15 yards linen cloath and 30 yards fine	1	10	0
	To my sonn Will for pention due Martinmass coming by Mr. Fenwick	30	0	0
	To my sonn Ned lent by Mr. Fenwick	30	0	0
	30. To Scremerston Willy Smith for drawing Branxton £11 rent charge	0	10	0
Nov.	1. To James Nesbett for his goods taken by Mr. Midford for suspition of felony and to repaire his damage all being cleered and discharged betwixt him and me	10	0	0
	4. To cosen Peggy Clavering for a night gowen for my wife	5	19	3
	To Nelly Hall for bringing my wife's night gowen	0	1	0
	To Mrs. Selbys[43] midwife of Beall by my wife	0	2	6
	For a dozen brass buttons to Mr. Edminson by Robert Simmons and Burgundy pitch	0	4	0
	7. To Scremerston Willy Smith for peruseing and reading the writing betwixt Mr. Salvine and selfe to nephew Charles Selby	0	3	4
	10. To the Fenwick smith for shooeing the coach horses since last Whittsonday	0	13	0
	To George Rose for 20 quarts brandy for my wife	2	5	0
	14. To sonn Hary and sonn John pentions by cosen Fleetwood	20	0	0
	15. To Robin Wilson smith for work at Buckton by Willy Smith	1	4	6

---

[43] Hannah Burrell, wife of William Selby of Beal. (R.N.D. 338).

Nov.	17.	To Luke Foster smith and cleered with him from Whittsonday '93 to martinmass '93 for maner of smith worke	2	10	2
		To my wifes charges att Mrs. Selby's crissening att Beall	0	5	0
	29.	To Scremerston Willy Smith for writings drawing by my wife	0	6	0
		To Jemmy Hann for killing beefes and meate to the house	0	8	0
Dec.	8.	To my wife to buy an ass with	1	1	0
		To Robert Simmons for a grey horse sadle and bridle	5	11	0
	11.	To sonn Hary for plush for brithes	1	0	0
	12.	To cosen Fleetwood to one in Ancroft for 20 yards of flannell for my wife	1	0	0
	14.	Lent Mrs. Strangways[44] and her sonn by bond	170	0	7
	18.	To Igg Maine and Beard for worke in the garden	0	9	8
	20.	To Mr. William Selby of Beall for Buckton Fenwick and Haggerston sess for the repaire of the south bridge in Haggerston	3	0	0

1693/4.

Jan.	2.	To Berrington sarvents and piper when wee all dined there	1	5	0
	17.	To sonn Ned by sonn Jacky aforehand rent[45]	60	0	0
	17.	To Mr. Peter Potts atturney for charge of passing Milkhouse Royall Rents Haggerston tyeths Island and houses Kyloe rentcharge Time in Durham Court	11	0	0
Feb.	3.	To Mary Ivison for helping to make waxe kandells	0	1	0
		To cosen Fleetwood by my wife's order for halfe years sallary now due	4	0	0

[44] Elizabeth Wilkie, widow of Edward Strangways of Cheswick.
[45] Rent for Hazelrigg.

Feb.	7.	To Cudy Midford for ingrossing Norham '93 Court Rowles [Rolls] and Rules and orders and streets of Court parchments for the year 1693	0	4	6
	9.	My wife att Fowbury to Mrs. Orde nurse and groome[46]	0	6	0
	14.	To cosen Fleetwood for treating cosen Peggy Headworth[47] at Barwick	0	18	0
		For 40 quarts sherry sack of my wife to cosen Clavering	2	13	4
	20.	To my wife for expenses at Mrs. Wilky's crissening	0	8	0
March	4.	To Preston skipper for bringing our Lenten provision by Anty Peacock	0	9	0
		To sonn Will in part of sallary	10	0	0
		To sonn Hary in part of sallary	3	0	0
	16.	To my cosen Fleetwood for cockles and lobsters	1	0	0
		To William Browen mason for faceing the old woman's wall in Barwick garden by cosen Fleetwood Butler	0	19	0

1694.

Apr.	3.	To cosen Fleetwood by my wife's order for spining corse yarne	0	12	0
	22.	To Robert Simmons for my house sess in Barwick house last quarter '93	0	4	6
		To Robert Simmons for Bullimor rent for Barwick house for '93	0	2	0
		To Robert Simmons for Barwick house water sprigg rent for '93	0	2	6
	26.	My charges att Twisell Bridge End with the Commissioners	0	4	0
		To Mr Chattoe for my suite and waistcoate and hatt band	13	0	0

---

[46] See Introduction, p. xiii.
[47] Probably Margaret daughter of Ralph Hedworth of Chester Deanery and Eleanor Lambton; now aged 17. (Surtees, Durham, II, 151.)

		To Wilson tayler for makeing suite and waistcoate with pocketts and other triming	1	10	0
May	4.	To the blind fiddler Cutty when son Ned's wife came home	0	6	0
	6.	For a silver cross with 2 stones to a Barwick sarjant by my wife	1	2	0
		To my wife for 30 quarters white wine att Couldstream by Anty Peacock	1	10	0
	12.	To John Robison piper when sonn Ned brought home his wife	0	3	4
	13.	To Watt Ashley for the repaire of 2 long wiggs	0	14	6
	25.	To Willt Steell for my part of Haselrigg for repaire of Chatton church	1	5	0
	26.	To Luke Forster cleering all smith worke down to this day	2	10	0
	30.	To Mr. Joseph Forster for all worke don to this day	3	18	9
June	2.	To cosen Clavering for her 21 boles of bigg for matt	13	13	0
		To sonn Hary halfe year annuity by cosen Fleetwood	10	0	0
		To sonn Jacky halfe years annuity by cosen Fleetwood	10	0	0
		To sonn Francis for Whittsonday '94 by Lady Charlton[48]	20	0	0
		To sonn Will for pockett monie by my wife and selfe	10	0	0
		To sonn Will halfe year pention '94	30	0	0
	11.	To an old Scotch woman for bleatchin 2 webbs cloath att Greyden by cosen Fleetwood	0	5	5
		My wifes charges with my daughter into the Hylands[49]	2	2	0
		To old Rayph Beednall for a bull calfe	0	12	0
	13.	To Willy Steel for the 2nd quarter's sess for 2 parts of Haselrigg due for son Ned Haggerston to pay	7	7	6

June	17.	To Cudy Read for cloath dyeing for my wife	0	9	6
		To Cudy Read for cleering all postage to this day	0	13	10
	18.	To Fillis Chartar widdow for a 3 year old black coult for the coach	6	0	0
	19.	To young Lowlin William Selby mother mortgage of £200 which with £400 before makes in all £600	200	0	0
		To young Carmichell's wedding by cosin Fleetwood for my wife and selfe	0	10	0
	19.	To Dolly and Alice Carnaby at Carmichell's wedding	0	7	6
	20.	To Sir Francis Tempest for his old white Galloway that I gave to Jack Fenwick	1	0	0
	21.	To Willy Smith for 3 futher peetts for my wife for stilling to a Lowick man	0	3	6
	26.	To cosen Carnabys[50] Gardiner by wife for bringing a baskett of cherries	0	1	0
		To Peggy Ruderford when she went to Foulden faire by cosen Fleetwood	1	10	0
	29.	To Tom Morton for 20 bols seed oates for Hazellrigg	7	10	0
	30.	To the webster for weaveing 4 webbs of linin cloath by cosen Fleetwood	1	6	2
July	4.	To old Mr. Anthony Counton, Barwick, for 6 trees by Willy Smith	2	2	0
	16.	To the Middleton gardiner when my wife and daughter was there	0	2	0
		To Tom Beednall and for a pound of sugar to treate my daughter and wife	0	2	0
	20.	To my sonn Will in part of his pention	5	0	0
		To Will Archbould in leu of not houlding Norham Corts for '93	5	0	0

---

[48] Mary, daughter of Sir Edward Widdrington of Cartington and widow of Sir Edward Charlton of Hesleyside. See introduction p. xi.

[49] The hill country of Northumberland: Callaly and Biddleston.

[50] Probably Mary, daughter of William Armorer of Midleton and widow of William Carnaby of Halton.

26 SIR THOMAS HAGGERSTON

Aug. 23. To the poor in Wooller left with Mrs. Chattoe to give amongst them — 0 1 0

1. To Mr. Sleigh of Goswick for this halfe yeer's Lamass rent for the pley [plea] ground betwixt Cheswick and Goswick payd by Willy Smith — 1 0 0

2. To cosen Fleetwood for her sallary — 4 0 0

7. To sonn Will for pockett monie — 20 0 0

13. For a bell; a paire of Kandlestick peuder and ladell att Grindon rigg — 0 12 6

15. To Short of Island for 4 firkins of Crowen soap by cosen Fleetwood — 4 0 0

22. To Andrew Jackson maltman of Berrington for sifting 25 kills of malt — 0 5 9

23. To Mr. John Wilky, Broomhouse, by order for his in law's use to cleer my wife's account to this day with Mr. Francis Brandling marchant in Neucastle[51] — 9 4 0

Sept. 6. To Mr. Medcalfe in charity by my wife — 1 0 0

To my sonn Hary for a belt and dagger by cosen Fleetwood — 0 18 0

To Jack Bell buttler for 2 quarter's and a halfe wage by cosen Fleetwood — 2 10 0

13. To Cudy Read for 35 stirks bought att Harbottle faire with all charges — 47 4 8

15. To Stuart pedler for lace for my wife — 1 6 0

Oct. 25. To Mrs. Edminson for six paire of Scotch hawks bells by Roger Maine — 0 19 4

29. My charges goeing and coming from Stella att Neucastle and Durham — 4 8 0

For 12 pound of chawing Tobaco att Mr. Lambs in Durham by Willy Smith — 1 16 0

To the castle garth quaker shoemaker for a paire of spring bootes — 0 11 0

29. For 2 prospective glasses att Neucastle faire — 0 3 6

For all horses shooeing at Chester in the street — 0 3 6

[51] See n.25.

		For 12 washballs 2s. for 12 sheets guilt paper 5d. for a spunge 7d. In all	0	3	0
		To Counceller Hary Lambton for several cases and opinions; saulved	3	6	0
Nov.	2.	To the glew makers in Chester for 1 stone glew	0	5	4
	8.	Robin's charges with the coach when he brought sonn Ned and wife home	1	1	11
	17.	Sonn Will half year pension by cosen Fleetwood	30	0	0
		Sonn Hary half year pension by cosen Fleetwood	10	0	0
		To young William Ollivant for plaistering 33 days in the Infirmiry	2	9	6
Dec.	14.	To sonn Jacky for his annuity due november 11 by cosen Fleetwood	10	0	0
	16.	To cosen Fleetwood for a paire of knit silke gartars	0	11	0

1694/5.

Jan.	22.	To Mr. Francis Brandling cleering all accounts and booke debts to the 10 Jan '94 by George Dunn upon my order	13	8	4
Feb.	9.	To Mr. Glover for painting my closet and other worke in the house with cullering severall picture frames	7	0	0
	11.	To my wife in charges att Mrs. Ord's labour att Fowburye	0	6	0
	22.	To Mr. Widdrington in charity by my wife	0	10	0
	22.	For 2 Callico aparrons for Dolly and Alice Carnaby	0	3	6
March	8.	To Mrs. Ord's nurse att Fowbury given by my wife	0	5	0
	9.	To Sir Marke Milbanke for releaseing his intrests to me of all Twisell estate with all the Northumberland estate;	102	0	0
		allso to Councellor Lambton for adviceing the best waye about it[52]	2	4	0

[52] See Introduction p. xiii.

	All my charges in goeing and coming from Neucastle and stayeing 4 days and nights or wee cud come to a resolution	4	8	0
	My charges to Great Ryle to meett Mr. Allgood where Sir William van Colster and Lady executed Sir Marke's lease and release to me of all the affoare estates	0	12	6
	To Mr. Allgood and his clark for draweing all leases and releases counterparts bonds receipts for writings as will apear by noates for the finishing all the securities relateing to the foresaid estates	11	7	8
March 23.	For Mr. Chattoe for 3 liveries coats briches waistcoates and a wide Coachman's coate with all maner of other trimings	13	12	10
	To Wilson, tayler for making the liveries 26s. and more triming 14s. In all	2	0	0
	To cosen Fleetwood for cockels Lent '94 for the house use	1	2	0
	To Dolly Carnaby for an Easter gift	0	3	0
24.	To my wife for a Vallantine gift to James Moore gardiner	0	10	0

1695.

28.	To 2 painted doe skinns for a paire of britches	0	16	0
April 8.	To the men that found the sea wrak Beacon hogshead and yard	0	6	0
13.	To Anty Peacock for charges to his last journey to Glascoe	0	14	0
15.	To the lobster men in Island for 22 cuple halfe of lobsters in Lent for the house use by cosen Fleetwood	0	11	3
21.	To Lady Charleton by bill from Nicholas Fenwick of Neucastle Alderman for sonn Francis aneuity due for '95	20	0	0
May 14.	(Pensions) Will by cosen Fleetwood	30	0	0
	Hary by cosen Fleetwood	10	0	0
	Jacky by cosen Fleetwood	10	0	0

June	6.	To cosen Hary Lambtons messenger about sonn Will's business of settlement[53]	0	12	0
	7.	To sonn Will by Jack Turbett aforehand rent	20	0	0
	15.	To Lady Morrison for sack sent by Sir John Cockeram payd her by Anty Peacock	9	0	0
		To Barwick Customers for tunage and cleering of James Gordon's ship with pease	1	2	0
	17.	To John Greyham carrier for bringing a side sadell and Twadell gardiner by cosen Fleetwood	0	2	6
		To Willy Steel for 2 quarters Hasellrigg land taxes '95	6	7	10
		To Willy Steel for 2 yeares Rogue monie	0	2	4
	17.	Contributed with sonn Ned and nephew Selby for service done by baylife Moffett of Wooller	0	10	0
	21.	For 89 yards halfe for damask and dyper att Edenburge for my wife by cosen Margaret Clavering scotch yard and measure	8	18	3
	26.	To Tom Staward high Cunstable for Goale monie for Hasellrigg	0	1	10
		To Tom Staward high Cunstable for Trophie monie for Hasellrigg	0	2	0
	28.	To Will Archbould in leu of houldin Norham corts for '95 but not payable till lammas	5	0	0
July	2.	To charges att Kyloe apealing to the Commissioners to no effect	0	8	0
	7.	To the Comissary Court att Anwick for church warden fees	0	9	0
		To Cudy Read for postage of letters to the date in the margent	ɔ	4	6

[53] His marriage settlement.

July	15.	To cosen Ellick Lambton[54] for six paire of hawkes bells from Edenburgh	0	10	0
	16.	To cosen Fleetwood for Jane Forster's spining wage with her comorade	1	1	0
	18.	For salt for the house use	1	0	0
		To my cosen Fleetwood for my wife's expenses at Mrs. Selby's crissening att Beall	0	6	0
	22.	To Mr. Midford's sarvants when my wife and I was att Norham	0	5	0
	25.	To Rayph Heath, Island, mason for wining one paire marble millstones	4	0	0
Aug.	27.	To cosen Harry Lambton for a fee att Durham about Mrs. Strangwayes' monie	1	10	0
		To cosen Hary Ridle in charity at Stella[55]	0	10	0
		To sonn Ned at Durham in part of Hazell-rigg '95 lammas Rent	30	10	0
		To a pedler for 33 yards of gerth webb at 2d. per yard	0	5	6
		To my wife given her nurse att Durham coming to see her	1	10	0
		To my wife given Mrs. Salkeld in charity att Bidleston	0	10	0
		To cosen Rayph Haggerston[56] att Stella by Willy Smith	5	0	0
		My wifes charges to Durham and what I lost att Ashett with things bought[57]	31	0	0
	31.	To Mr. Cudbert Midford for two acers of land in Norham bought of	12	8	0
		To Willy Smith for boateing over at Neu-burne 18d. to the groome att Witton 1s. to the soldiers att Island fort 5s. to the poore 6d. for ringing wyre 8d. In all	0	8	2

[54] Brother of Henry Lambton; see n.30.

[55] Probably Henry Riddell son of Sir Wm. Riddell of Gateshead (d.1654/5) and Katherine, daughter of Sir Henry Widdrington.

[56] Ralph Haggerston of Berwick, gent. was returned as a Papist in 1680 HMC House of Lords *op. cit.*).

[57] Eshott was the home of Wm. Carr (1658-1738) and Jane, daughter of Col. Wm. Strother of Fowberry.

Sept.	2.	To John Winlowe, Island, for 40 great salt fish 29s. for 40 little fish 2s. and for 20 ling 19s. and for 10 fish 6s. 6d. In all by Willy Smith	2	16	6
	9.	To Tom Pawlins wife for 12 geese at 6d. per peece praysed	0	12	0
	27.	To Jane Barbar my wife's drye nurse in charity by my wife	1	10	0
	27.	To sonn Jacky for a maile trunk by cosen Fleetwood	0	10	0
	28.	To Betty Ellison and her daughter for 29 days sheering by Willy Smith	0	14	6
		To Mr. Glen in part of staire case worke don by Willy Smith	8	10	0
Oct.	3.	To sonn Will upon acount of his first rents beginning Whittsonday '95	100	0	0
		For 53 wedders att Wooler faire by Jemmy Hann	19	15	3
	16.	To Will Chattoe for a paper of horse cordiall by Roger Maine	0	1	0
	20.	For 9 boles of Cleevland seed wheat 16.2.6 for charges in bringing it 20s.	17	2	6
	24.	To John Maitland for a cast of Fawkons and bringing them from Edenburge	6	0	0
	25.	To son Will sent to Dillston by Roger Maine upon acount	30	0	0
		To John Mautland marchant att the head of Black Fryer Wind in Edenburge for one paire of Doggskinn Gloves for a Fawkner	4	0	0
Nov.	2.	To Mrs. Hanna Selby of Beall for 40 dryed cod fish by Willy Smith			
	7.	To the Barwick waites att sonn Will's wife coming home by Cosen Fleetwood	0	10	0
	14.	. . . Son Harry . . . son Jacky annuities	20	0	0
	18.	To my wife; her godson Tomy Selby halfe a ginnie given	0	15	0
	29.	To Cosen Clavering of Berrington for her part of pease sould att Neucastle	20	0	0

Dec.	1.	To Peter Potts by bill to Mr. Fenwick to pay Hudleston writer for time came hither for my wife £10.2.7 and for several done himselfe £17.11.8 In all	27	14	3
	21.	To mr. Tho. Grevie Barwick for 4 bottles of Clarett for the house use	0	6	8
	23.	To Doctour Coper and Mr. Patrick Smith for sarveing the five Cures due last Michellmass 1695 sallieries	25	0	0
	24.	To cosen Bridgett Buttler [58] by bill to York from Alderman Fenwick	4	0	0
	27.	To Igg Maine for looking to the Hawkes	0	2	6
	28.	To George Rye miller in Bellford for a grey gelding by Roger Maine	6	17	0

1695/6.

Jan.	10.	To Mr. Ogle of Cawsey parke for 48 spoaks for coach wheels by Jemy Wilkyson	0	11	0
		To William Frissell, Ancroft, for 24 qrts halfe Brandy by cosen Fleetwood	2	8	2
	23.	To Cosen Alexander Lambton for the last Clapbord for the staire case	17	10	0
Feb.	4.	Charges att Midleton with my wife and daughters	0	2	0
	20.	To the bungler smoaky chimney Curer Norham maisson	0	8	0
March	1.	To Robin maisson for my wifes chimney by Cosen Fleetwood	0	2	0
		To one Carrier that brought the first oyster by Cosen Fleetwood	0	1	0
	6.	To Robin maisson for my wifes chamber chimney by Cosen Fleetwood	0	1	0
	19.	To Mr. Glen for makeing the staire case	29	5	0
		To his 2 men given that wrought with him Will Grey and John Tunstall	0	10	0

1696.

Apr.	13.	To my wife for a valantine gift to sonn Hary	1	10	0

[58] Sister of Fleetwood.

Apr.	23.	To Counceller Lambton for Fees att Morpeth concerbing Lowick affaires	1	10	0
		To charges att meetting Mr. Charles Howard att Morpeth [59]	0	18	0
May	7.	To William Short Island for 4 days worke for my wife	0	4	0
	11.	To Davison weaver of Ancroft for 35 yards working for my wife's use by cosen Fleetwood	0	9	0
	15.	To Mr. Glover for 15 paire of window shutters painting and some other worke	8	5	0
	18.	To the weaver's wife of Barmore for 18 yards Linnen weaveing my wife	0	2	6
	20.	To a Twisell man for 30 hanks of fine yarne for my wife by cosen Fleetwood	1	8	0
	31.	To Scremerston Willy Smith for engrossing my last will and Testament and some other things[60]	1	0	0
June	1.	For wood vessell att Weettwood faire for my wife's use by Dolly Carnaby	1	3	0
	6.	To the Comesary Cort for Haggerston, Fenwick and Buckland Church wardon Fees	0	9	6
	14.	To Cudy Read for takers lappers and Clippers of 58 scoare sheep	1	6	6
	18.	To my wife for midwife nurse and groome att Felkington[61]	0	11	0
	26.	(Annuities to sons Harry & Jacky)	20	0	0
July	9.	To Goswick gardner with my wife and daughter to eate cherries	0	6	0
	10.	To Fenwick and Buckton mowers 18 days by Willy Smith	0	18	0
	12.	To Lowick carrier for goods bought my wife from Mr. Francis Brandling	0	9	6
	14.	To Mr. John Maittland for a cast of			

[59] Of Overacres; son of James Howard of Redesdale and Dorothy Errington of Bingfield; married 8 December, 1687, Eleanor daughter of Sir Francis Blake of Ford, and widow of George Selby of Twisell.

[60] Will dated 1 August, 1695.

[61] Mrs. Mary Ord née Strother; the child, Jane, was baptized 18 June, 1696 (Norham reg.).

		Fawcons six pound and for a cast Tarsett Gentles £3 Jack Turbetts charges bringing one cast 10s. for the other cast a Footmans charge from Edenburge in bringing them hither 8s. In all (sic)	10	18	0
July	15.	To a pedler for 5 yards muslan for my Apron and 2 crevatts by cosen Fleetwood	1	5	8
	16.	To Gingerman 2 stawkes of sealing waxe 6d. and one pound of haire powder 1s.	0	1	6
Aug.	17.	Charges goeing and coming to Neucastle Assiess	2	15	0
		Charges for Treatings of business in Taverns	0	12	0
		To a Cuttler for a swoard	0	10	0
		For a paire of Gold and silver weights	0	5	0
		For things bought my wife by my daughter Mary Haggerston[62]	2	8	8
		For a neu Fashiond bridle	0	4	6
		To Councell for severall Fees	8	16	0
	17.	To 2 witness Fees for goeing and coming from Neucastle	1	0	0
		their charges and horses att Neucastle	1	3	0
Sept.	8.	To men in the Island for 40 cuple of salt fish for cosen Thorneton[63]	1	16	0
		To the Lowick carrier for Carrage of the fish to Witton: 24 stone weighing	0	8	0
	9.	To the old payver for paveing 600 yards att 2d. per yard	5	0	0
		To Ned Wilson tayler for makeing my gold fringed black wastcoate and coate	0	10	0
	11.	To Mr. Peter Potts in discharge of all accounts 'twixt him and me to this day	53	0	0
		To Mr. Peter Potts to returne to London for sonn Frank's and wife's use	40	0	0
		To Mr. Robert Widdrington in charity by my wife	0	10	0

[62] Wife of Edward Haggerston.
[63] Nicholas Thornton of Netherwitton.

Sept.	20.	For 60 wedders of Mr. George Colling-wood of Murton att St. Rinion faire by Cudy Read and Tom Smith price £24: for 40 wedders of Mr. Joseph Orde of Longeridge 15.15.0 att St. Rinion faire by Cudy Read and Tom Smith with toule and sives and Riddes and other charges 0.11.1 In all	40	6	1
Oct.	5.	To my wife for bookes bought of Margaret Gorswidge by cosen Fleetwood	0	8	4
	8.	To Mr. Cudbert Midford for charges in passing Mr. Francis Reeds fine for Kyloe	5	15	0
	12.	To William Sinkler of Lowick for traine band soldier and coate and Armes to '96	0	16	10
	15.	To Chattoe pedler for 3 paire washt leather Riding gloves	0	3	0
	16.	To Mrs. Story for knitting 2 paire stockings for my wife by cosen Fleetwood	0	4	0
	17.	To Mr. Edminston for trees to the Island houses repaireing and building houses	1	4	0
		To Cosen John Clavering for £300 intrest due 19 8br. 96	9	0	0
	20.	Lent Mrs. Selby of Lowlin to paye her father in law Mr. Hary Ord of Holly Island a year's anuety due last lamass 96	6	0	0
	27.	Given to Alice Carnaby att her goeing to Dilston	0	6	0
Nov.	16.	My wifes charges to Dilston goeing and returning by cosen Fleetwood	11	17	0
		(Annuities Harry & John)	20	0	0
		My wifes charges att Mrs. Selbye's sickness of Beall by cosen Fleetwood	0	3	6
		For Cloaths att London bought by cosen Plowden for my wife	26	14	0
		Sent by my wife by bill to cleer sonn Francis aneuity	6	14	0
		and towards the next years aneuity payd	2	14	0
	18.	To the Cooper for wage due martinmas 96 by cosen Fleetwood	0	11	6

		To the Cooper for mending 2 hawkes batheing Tubbs by cosen Fleetwood	0	1	0
Nov.	18.	To Willy Smith for bootes and shoes for Robert Simmon's postillion	0	10	6
	26.	To my daughter Mary Haggerston for things bought my wife	6	9	6
Dec.	1.	To cosen Fleetwood salt since Feb. '95 to this day	1	7	6

1696/7.

Jan.	1.	In Neu Year's gifts by my wife and selfe by cosen Fleetwood	19	14	0
	24.	To a pedler att Berrington for 5 yards halfe lace for shirts ruffels	0	12	6
March	6.	To sonn Ned in part of Hazelrigg halfe year's '96 Kandelmass rent	50	0	0
	22.	Lent Adam Lamb to pay his glass windowe sess by Willy Smith	0	2	0
		Lent Adam Lamb to bury his wife with by cosen Fleetwood	0	15	0

1697.

	27.	To Roger Maine for his coach black maire to cleer her price	5	0	0
		To Tomy Selby and little Charles given by my wife[64]	0	16	0
Apr.	2.	For 500 bricks to Tweedmouth brick-burners by Anty Peacock	0	4	0
	20.	To Clarke for stateing and pointing Barwick house[65]	2	10	0
	23.	Lent sonn Ned in dollors acounted and crost X	20	0	0
		To Robin Atkine mason for 10 days worke att my daughter's closett	0	10	0
	23.	To Mr. George Wytham of Cliff[66] for 3 coach-mares by Robin Simmons	25	5	0

[64] Children of Charles Selby of Biddleston.

[65] Severely damaged by fire in 1687.

[66] Second and eldest surviving son of William Wytham of Cliffe N.R.Y. and Anne, daughter of George Collingwood of Eslington, Northumberland, and Dalden, co. Durham; d. 1703.

	27.	To Tom Beadnall for doggs from August for the Hawks	0	10	4
	30.	To Willy Smith for charges to Durham to the Commissioners	0	4	0
May	3.	To Willy Smith for safferan for my wife	0	5	0
		To Mrs. Ashley for makeing the missall regester	0	5	0
	7.	To my wife for buying a booke of phisick	0	9	8
	10.	To Mrs. Margaret Selby of Lowlin for 36 weders at 8s. per weder bought by Jamy Hann	14	8	0
	14.	To Bessy . . . for 5 cuple of lobsters for the house use by cosen Fleetwood	0	2	6
		To Mrs. Ann Selby of Beall for 40 dyed fish payd her husband	1	10	0
	17.	To George Rose for meate to the house and hawkes beefe	5	7	9
	19.	Lent Luke Forster Berrington smith by cosen Fleetwood	2	0	0
		To Adam Smith for £500 intrest due last november '96 by Willy Smith	30	0	0
	24.	To George Clarke Neucastle carryer for 36 stone of goods brought my wife from Neucastle cleering all to this day by cosen Fleetwood	0	15	0
		To my sonn Hary for Whittson anuity by cosen Fleetwood	10	0	0
	28.	To sonn Jacky for Whittson anuity by cosen Fleetwood	10	0	0
	28.	To my wife att Mrs. Wilky's crissening to midwife nurse and pyper	0	11	0
June	1.	To Mary Ivisson for a quarter's cookeing by cosen Fleetwood	0	15	0
		To little Tomson for undercookeing by cosen Fleetwood	0	4	9
		To cosen Fleetwood for London letter to Jemmy Crawford	0	0	3
		To Nealson shooemaker for shooes and slipers for my wife by cosen Fleetwood	0	13	3

June	3.	To cosen Fleetwood Buttler by my wife's order for the use of the poore	0	5	0
	8.	To Lowick Carrier Clarke for bringing the cooke from Neucastle	0	8	0
	16.	To Mr. Francis Brandling marchant in Neucastle in part of goods due	60	0	0
	25.	To Thomas Moore for Haggerston proportion of Church sess for the repaire of the Holly Island church	0	15	0
	29.	To Igg Maine allowed in his rent for 4 veale cawlfes for the house use	2	0	0
		To cosen Rayph Haggerston for 4 coach glasses £4.15; to cleer with Mr. Dyer for neuse letters last halfe yeare ending June the first '97, £2; and to my [cosen?] Mrs. Margery Haggerston in charity £2.5; All returned by Alderman Fenwick	9	0	0
July	6.	To the Lady Morryson for sugar and spices for my wife by Willy Smith	2	5	2
		For a paire of Callaly waine wheels for Buckton	1	10	0
	18.	For 22 yards of fine meuriceland cloath att 2s. per yard	2	4	0
	26.	To Cudy Read for cliping 3 score scores and 13 scores of sheep	1	10	0
		To Jack Dixson for 2 paire of edenburgh hawkes bells	0	4	0
		To a woman of Lowlin for bleatching 60 yards of cloath by coseh Fleetwood	0	5	0
	29.	For whallboane and buckroom 12s. and for makein my wife's stayes by moyses by cosen Fleetwood	1	0	4
Aug.	2.	To Ford sarvants when my wife, sonn Will, cosen Fleetwood and I dined there	0	10	0
		To young Bryan Grey's first daughters crissening my wife's charges there	0	10	0
		To Felkington midwife and nurse by my nurse and groome	0	12	0

Aug.	19.	To weaving 21 yards of Fine Hucka-back by cosen Fleetwood	0	10	6
		For bletching 13 webbs of Cloath in Scotland by cosen Fleetwood	0	6	4
	27.	To the keeper of Chillingham and his man for a Fouch of veneson bringing	0	7	6
	29.	To Cudy Read for charges att Whittingham faire	0	2	6
	30.	To cosen Hary Lambton for fee halfe a ginnie	0	11	0
		For 3 neu fassioned musslan cravatts	1	8	0
		To the quaker shooemaker for 2 paire of my shooes by Willy Smith	0	9	0
		For six paire of gloves for myselfe by Willy Smith	0	12	0
		For washballs for shaveing by Willy Smith	0	3	8
		For 2 paire brass kandellsticks 4 snuffers and 2 panns by Willy Smith	0	17	6
		For peares and charges att Shotton edge	0	8	0
		To Neucastle musick	0	2	6
		To sarvants where I lodged	3	11	0
		The large of sarvants and horses in Neucastle	1	15	0
	30.	To William Chambers in earnest for building a horse and winde mill	0	3	0
		To William Munkcaster a drover for 2 oxen and 5 cowes for feeding	15	0	0
Sept.	2.	To Roger Maine for catching 46 ratts att a penny a ratt	0	3	6
		To Buckton satcher for satching Norham house att 12d. a day	0	7	0
	4.	To the gingerman for 4 pound of sweet powder haire	0	4	0
		To Tom Allbourne for cullering my daughter Haggerston's closett	1	1	0
	9.	To Mr. Tho. Bowelby sadler for all things belonging to a suite of coach harness for six horses	25	0	0
	12.	To the 4 ewe milkers by cosen Fleetwood	0	16	0

	To Cudy Reads nurse and midwife att his daughter Barbara's crissening	1	0	0
	To the pavers att halfe pence the yard with their dyett	0	11	9
Sept. 25.	To a cloakebagg and Gilly cranky night gowne[67] To Rowly Braythwaite by Roger Maine	1	10	0
28.	Mr. Thomas Clavering of Bousden for a young horse Roger Maine sould to pay for him at Martinmass '96 in Haggerston house[68]	2	15	0
Oct. 2.	To my godson Tom Smith att Hillhead[69]; given an English crawen	0	5	0
5.	To William Smith of Hillhead for examining Sir Francis Tempest's acounts given in by George Dunn and George Lawes for the yeare 1696	0	5	0
	To cosen Betty Plowden[70] att the Golden Fleece against St. Pawle's church returned by George Dunn to her for sonn Francis aneuity due last Whittsonday '96 £17.6.0 and cosen Margery £2.14.0 In all	20	0	0
7.	To my Lady Morryson for fruit and salt by Robert Simmons	4	15	0
9.	To Gilbert Clarke for slateing worke att neds house in Buckton	12	15	0
	To the getters of the fogg for the slates instead of lime	0	19	6
	To the smith for all kinds of nailes for the roofe and house	2	6	0
	For 60 dailes for latts and other uses about the roof and house	3	0	0
	For leading slates from the Island to Buckton house 20 futher	3	0	0

---

[67] Was this a fashion named for the battle of Killiecrankie, 9 years earlier?

[68] Thomas Clavering was perhaps a son of William Clavering of Bowsden and his wife Dorothy Selby (m. 8 August, 1671).

[69] Scremerston.

[70] Named as niece in the will of Margaret Thornton of Witton Shields, 5 February, 1700/1; usual agent in the transfer of Haggerston funds to London.

		For all kind of labouring and saweing of lattes			
		To Robert Atkin maison for cureing the chimney of smoak and beame fitting 8 days	0	12	0
		To Robert Attkin maison in part of worke att Smyfield sonn Ned's house[71]	3	0	0
Oct.	16.	To Tom Allburne for plaistering my daughter's closett and kitching	1	7	0
		To cosen Fleetwood for her faireing att Neucastle a paire of laced shooes	0	6	2
	17.	Spent at Wooler Haugh head with Mr. Armorer and Lance Aullgood[72]	0	6	6
		Spent with Sir Francis Blake and at Eatall[73]	0	2	0
		To Willy Smith Cudy Reed's and other charges in vewing Ellingham	0	4	0
	22.	To charges att Bellford meeting Mr. Armorer and prockter	0	3	6
	28.	To cosen Peggy Clavering for night gowne petty coate gloves and gartars for wife att Neucastle faire	5	11	10
		To Margaret Gorswidge for bookes and other things bought by my wife	0	7	2
Nov.	6.	To Tom Ashley as a Godband gift by Robin Simmons	0	5	0
	11.	Sons Hary and Jacky martinmass pentions	20	0	0
	14.	To Dolly and Alice Carnaby for a quarter's wage now due	1	5	0
		To Dolly and Alice Carnaby at parting each 5s.	0	10	0
	20.	To Anty Peacock for a little cowe to feed but dyed by Willy Smith	1	11	0
Dec.	4.	To John Pigg and Joseph Ord for Barwick house Bullimors Rent and watersprigg			

---

[71] Smeafield or Smithfield, near Buckton.

[72] First negotiations for purchase of Ellingham.

[73] Home of William Carr (d.1714/15). He married, the following year, Mary daughter of Wm. Carr of Eshott and Jane Strother.

for 2 years ending at Michellmass '96
by Betty Blacklock   0 9 0

Dec. 10. To Jemmy Crawford for dyeing my wife 2
paire stockens by cosen Fleetwood   0 1 0

13. To Mr. Richard Selby for 20 scoare firr
dailes att £4.10.0 per cent.   [sic]   15 0 0

16. To Joseph Ord for 5 years arears of
Bullimers rent due Michellmass '96 for
the fallen house bought of Singleton In
Barwick by my garden side   0 2 6

30. To my wife att Mrs. Selbye of Beall crissening of her daughter Nanny   0 15 0

1697/8.

Jan. 8. To Coll. Hyde in charity by my wife   1 0 0

14. To Jack Turbett for tayllering my coate
and waistcoate by cosen Fleetwood   0 0 10

For 3 dozen boottons att Neucastle by
George Clarke of Lowick carryer   0 1 9

Feb. 9. To my daughter's nurse and midwife by
my wife and selfe by cosen Fleetwood[74]   4 0 0

12. For 2 anchours of canary and clarett
£4.4.0 for 11 quarters of brandy
£0.18.4; for raaysons; currens; prunes;
figgs; 4 dozen oranges and lemons and
all sorts of spyces with barrells and
canvass baggs 8.11.0 In all   13 13 4

For a quire of good writing paper 7d.
and a quire of guilt paper 10d. In all   0 1 5

Anty's charges with 2 horses going to
Edenburgh and coming from it   0 10 7

For 20 quarters canary and 10 quarters
brandy by cosen Fleetwood   2 3 4

24. To Will Steel for sonn Ned's part of
Bridge sess of Hazellrigg by acquittance
in '97   0 9 10

March 2. To Mr. Michaell Medcalfe for a silver
crisem crissening oyle boxe   1 2 0

---

[74] This and the following entries refer to the birth of William Haggerston's son
Carnaby, eventual heir to Sir Thomas.

March 19.	To my wife's use returned to neece dowager Selby[75] to London by George Dunn		13	0	0

1698.

Apr. 5.	To charges att Mrs. Wood's Buriall att Preston[76]		0	2	6
	Lent the Corporation of Barwick upon a seven years bargin in gold		200	0	0
15.	To John Luke in Lowick for 60 truss of hather for Berrington malt kiln		1	0	0
	To the Irish Barwick silver smith for cutting my steele seale and making a silver picks		1	0	0
May 9.	Lent Mr. John Forster of Barwick upon bond and judgment by the two Willy Smiths		20	0	0
14.	To sonn Ned for Smithfield martinmass '97 rent upon George Rose acount		17	0	0
	To sonn Ned for fruit trees sent my wife		0	8	0
	To Mr. Houseman for nephews and neece Selbye pictures payd by sonn Ned		4	0	0
	To Mr. Nicholas Fenwick for carrage of 2 boxes from London		0	6	4
	To Mr. Nicholas Fenwick to cost and charges of a blew millston from Rotterdam		27	0	0
16.	To cosen Fleetwood for glasses and cruitts		0	10	0
	To the glass man in charity by my wife for his broaken glasses by a fall		0	2	6
18.	To the Lady of Morrisson for 3 horse loades of salt being 11 Winchester bussell		1	5	6
28.	My wife's charges with my daughters att Wooller		0	2	0

---

[75] Ann Selby née Lumsden, widow of Thomas Selby (died s.p. 1684) elder brother of Charles Selby.

[76] Mary Armorer of Hoppen, widow first of Francis Brandling of Hoppen and secondly of Thomas Wood of Burton. Her son purchased the estate of Preston, which he had previously held as tenant, in 1717.

June	31.	To Nany Johnson's sonn's weding in Kenstone	0	10	0
	9.	To Watt Ashley for fraught of chariott axeltrees and wheels from London to Barwick	0	17	10
		To cosen Rayph Haggerston for a sett of chariott wheels and iron axel trees	8	11	8
		To cosen Rayph Haggerston for his pains and charges about the wheels	1	10	0
	12.	. . . sonn Hary annuity by cosen Fleetwood	10	0	0
		. . . sonn Jacky annuity by cosen Fleetwood	10	0	0
	23.	To the boate men Feast of corps cristy day[77] in holy Island by Hary Robison	0	10	0
		To sonn Francis for his aneuity due Whitt-sonday '98 and sent him by Cosen Plowden part of the £50 returned by Mr. Lance Ord[78] for me	20	0	0
	25.	To treate cosen Ann Lambton[79] in Barwick house by cosen Fleetwood	0	13	6
	29.	To Ned Wilson tayler for my suite and Willy Simmon's livery	0	18	0
	30.	To cosen Plowden for things for my wife and little Carnaby out of the £50 returned by Lance Ord of Weetwood	30	0	0
July	4.	To Tom Robison for toule[80]; charges with corne to Morpeth and Anwick	0	6	5
	7.	To Mrs. Horsburgh of Wooller for 4 dozen of clarett wine by Anty Peacock	2	16	0
	12.	Lost att cards by my wife and selfe to the Fowbury companie[81]	1	3	6
		To charges att Could Martin Tarne with Fowbury companie	0	8	0
	14.	To my Godson Tom Howard five guinies	5	10	0
	26.	To Mrs. Sara Hudson for a diamond ring by Willy Smith	10	0	0

[77] The summer festival of Holy Island; a relic of monastic days.
[78] Of Weetwood, son of William Ord of Berwick (d.1653) and Elizabeth daughter of Lancelot Strother; married in 1680 Margaret Eden, widow.
[79] Eldest daughter of Henry Lambton and sister of Barbara Clavering.
[80] i.e. toll.
[81] The Strother family.

		To Mr. Houseman for cosen Jeffords[82] pictur draweing and death heads by cosen Fleetwood	3	0	0
July	28.	To William Simin an old man 85 years of age in charity	0	5	0
	29.	To Robin Cooke for a tunn of flatt iron	14	0	0
Aug.	6.	To the Calalee wheelmaker for 2 paire of wheels by Tom Robyson	3	0	0
		To Ned Wilson for makeing plush britches by cosen Fleetwood	0	3	4
	10.	To George Clarke, Lowick carryer, to deliver Mr. Fenwick maire for John Blythman for a pad sadle with all furniture for myselfe by cosen Fleetwood	3	1	6
	28.	To Mr. Francis Brandling marchant in Neucastle for all goods my [wife] hath of him cleering all to the 25 of this August '95 [98] as by his acquittance upon a generall noote had and payd by Jemmy Crawford	38	9	6
	28.	More to Mr. Francis Brandling upon the same account by bill	11	0	0
	31.	To cosen Fleetwood for 36 quarters of sherry sack for my wifes use	1	16	0
Sept.	9.	To cosen Fleetwood for 12 quarters of Clarett wine	0	12	0
		To cosen Fleetwood for 20 quarters of Brandy for my wifes use	1	16	8
		To Mr. Charles Jackson for 2 hoggsheads of clarett wine by Robert Simmons	14	2	9
	15.	To the ginger man for one pound sweete haire powder	0	1	0
		To the hyreing the four coblemen of the Island for a yeare by Hary Robison	0	5	0
	17.	To Mr. Peter Potts for getting my sword dresst at London	1	2	6

[82] Mary daughter of William Armorer of Belford and Middleton, and widow of William Carnaby of Halton, remarried Fitzmaurice Gifford (SS. CXXXI, 126 f.n.). She is probably the person referred to as "cousin Carnaby" in the entry of 26 June, 1694.

Sept.	28.	To cosen Fleetwood for bee wax 2s for mouse traps 18d. for neuse letters 9d. In all	0	4	3
Oct.	2.	To Doctor Hume for advice to my wife 4 dollors and to George Smith for leting her blood	1	5	0
	6.	To Sir Francis Blake 10 guinies and Mrs. Howard 10 guinies given them by Mr. Peter Potts att passing Lowick fine to me	22	11	0
	31.	To the Scotch Cheswick schoollmaister for binding the holly court silvnius morgan attarld [sic] book and all the three scripturs by cosen Fleetwood	0	10	0
Nov.	12.	(Annuities to sons Henry and John £10 each)	20	0	0
	23.	To Charles Jackson of Barwick for 2 white mettle shaveing basons by cosen Fleetwood	0	2	8
	28.	To Jemmy Crawford for one pound of waxe booke candells	0	1	6
	30.	To William Frissell of Ancroft for 18 quarters of canary sack	1	7	0
		To William Frissell of Ancroft for 38 quarters of cherry sack	2	4	4
Dec.	10.	To my charges in the highlands waiteing of the young lady of Callalee[83]	0	12	6
		To eleven priests to pray for Sir Francis Tempest deceast at Monpiler the 6 of November 1698; acording to England's acounts given 11 ginies	12	2	0
	16.	To Ford groome at Mr. James Howard funerall[84]	0	1	0
	18.	To Mr. Person[85] to pray for Sr. Francis Tempest deceast att Monplier the 6 of November 1698 in France a ginny	1	2	0

[83] Anne daughter of William second Lord Widdrington and wife of John Clavering.

[84] See n. 59.

[85] Rev. Thomas Pearson, S.J. then at Durham.

Dec.	24.	To Gilbert Clarke for slateing and tyleing Barwick house	4	0	0
		To Tom Murton for carpingter worke at Barwick house the same time	0	12	0

1698/99.

Jan.	2.	To Coll. Hyde in charity by my wife	1	0	0
	15.	My charges to Neucastle too and froe when sonn Ned payd for Ellingham	3	5	0
		To Mrs Isabella Trumbull for washing laces and comodes for my wife by Tom Beadnell[86]	1	0	0
	30.	To Willy Hann of Couldburn for Mr. Wirge's composition due Wooller faire in '98	1	2	4
		To Willy Hann for Church sess 1s. 10d. cowe sess due in '98 for the land there 1s. 10d. land tax due 24 Dec. last 15s. In all	0	18	8
	30.	To William Staward and John Short collectors Haggerston with tyeth and the mills and land taxe for 2 last qrtrs in '98	13	18	8
		To William Staward for Haggerston part for Ancroft church books	0	1	3
		To the collectors for Fenwick and Buckton land tyeths mills malt barne and kill sess in '98	6	2	7
Feb.	1.	To Robert Simmons for a year's wage	5	0	0
		To Willy Simmons postilion year's wage	2	10	0
	2.	To Ned Wilson tayler for making my riding coate of my wife's spining by cosen Fleetwood	1	0	0
	3.	To Roger Maine for a year's wage	5	0	0
		For a paire of shooes for my wife in Barwick	0	3	0
	10.	To Mrs. Elinor Howard of Ford for passing a fine for Lowick to me by Mr. Peter Potts	11	0	0

[86] The commode was the frame over which the lady's curls were arranged.

Feb.	24.	To William Frissell of Ancroft for 8 yards damask; for 22 yards damask; 20 yards dyper and 19 yards dyper all scotch measur for my wife's use	5	15	6
March	20.	To cosen Fleetwood for my wife's pockett monie	1	0	0
	22.	To the gingbread man for 2 pounds gingbread 12; orrangs; and 11 pound sweete powder	0	14	0

1699.

	25.	To my niece Jan Tempest which she gave in charity to her cosen Salkild	1	0	0
	30.	To Will Chattoe for a cloath hatt by cosen Fleetwood	0	10	0
		To Will Chattoe for 4 peeces of flowerd callico for my wife	3	1	0
Apr.	5.	To the 2 ministers for serving the 5 chapelys due this 25 March last	25	0	0
	7.	To my sonn Francis his anuity payd for all '98 ending Whittsonday '99	20	0	0
May	7.	To my wife for her Godson Frank Reed by cosen Fleetwood	0	5	0
	28.	To nurse Steell by my wife and selfe by cosen Fleetwood	1	3	6
June	1.	To George Smith for Munkrige securering our cuntry for theft my part	2	16	2
	6.	(Sons Hary & John annuities £10 each)	20	0	0
	15.	To charges with my wife and sister Salvin[87] att Fowbury and Weetwood	0	2	6
	29.	To Mrs. Strangway's wedding at Tweedmouth by cosen Fleetwood	0	10	0
July	3.	To Mr. Robert Cooke for a shipload of Raff Timber from Norraway	90	0	0
		To the maister for 2 greatt firr planks 10s. and to the sailors 20s. for 40 dails In all	1	10	0
	4.	To my wife given Ellingham gardiner for strawbiries and cherries	0	2	6

[87] Mary Clavering of Callaly, wife of Gerard Salvin of Croxdale, whose daughter Mary had married Sir Thomas's son.

July	5.	To Ned Wilson for makeing my moorning for Coll. Strother[88]	1	6	0
	7.	To cosen Fleetwood for 6 bols of salt att thr doore	1	14	0
		To cosen Fleetwood for a firrking of soape at Fenham	0	18	0
	10.	To Lord Widdrington keeper for venison 5s. and his man that brought it 2s. In all	0	7	0
	27.	To the Island for 40 cuple of salt fish for cosen Thornton with carrage by Willy Smith	2	12	0
	29.	To sonn Hary in charity for a suit of church stuff	1	12	0
Aug.	4.	In our jurney to Bidleston	2	6	0
	10.	To Hary Robison for looking a fisherman to make up 4 for my boate	0	0	?
	11.	To Rayph Redhead Island for 90 codfish and 10 ling by Willy Smith	4	2	6
		To George Smith for houlding Norham 2 Courts in '98	6	12	6
		To George Smith for houlding Lowick Court in '98	1	18	0
Sept.	4.	To Adam Bell for cobling a paire of shooes to make them easy by Willy Kellett	0	2	6
	12.	To Doctor Home for a mouse cullerd Gallowaye 6 ginnies	6	9	0
	17.	To old Will Archbould by his tenent Will King a yearly token during life	5	0	0
		[At St. Rinian's fair] 8 yards of cuntry russet cloath	0	16	3
		7 yards harden	0	5	0
		suies piggins and peares	0	1	2
		bee waxe	0	11	4
Oct.	1.	To Mr. Walter Ashley for floating Rob. Cooke's timber to Tweedmouth	0	5	3
	2.	To Mathew Forster by Mr. Counter's order mayer for '99 Cheswick six part of corne tyeth belonging to Barwick corporation payd by Tom Beadnell	9	0	0

[88] Buried 5 July, 1699 (N.C.H.N. XI, 134).

			£	s	d
Oct.	4.	To Robert Mauffland for a yeare and a halfe tyeth fish due '99 Martinmass of my fisher boate in the holy Island and allowed by Willy Smith	1	2	6
		To Robert Mauffland for 6 years' quitt rent for my house in the holy Island due for '99 and cleered till then by Willy Smith	0	8	0
	5.	To Robert Simmons' charges with my wife's cheeses gooing and coming from Stella	0	9	0
	9.	To Clark caryer of Lowick for bringing Troth Stoker	0	8	0
	13.	To Mathew Sibbitt of Longe Dykewall collector for '99 land taxes for Ancroft chapellry for Haggerston land for the 2 first quarters taxes £10.7.2 for the tyeth £1.5.8; for the 2 mills £2.5.10 In all	13	18	8
		To William Davison of Fennick Colectour for '99 land taxes for Kyloe chapellry for halfe of Fenwick land and all Buckton for the two first quarter's taxes with tyeths	11	12	5
		To Rayph Watson of Fenham Collectour for '99 land taxes for Holly Island chapellry for halfe of millhouseland for the first two quarters	2	5	10
	27.	To sonn John for '99 halfe year's anuity due that martinmass to come	10	0	0
Nov.	7.	To Mrs. Aspinwell midwife by my wife and selfe	2	7	0
	18.	To Ned Cooke by my wife's order to Jane Barbar's buriall a ginny	1	1	6
		To the Collectours of the windowe sess for '98 by Willy Smith	0	10	0
	24.	To sonn Ned for fruitt trees 16s. for packing up and carrage 2s. in all	0	18	0
	24.	(Wages: Tom Mudy, harvest; Tom Dunkin, cooper; Tom Blake, cowherd; Robin Wood, Willy Smith; John Bell, butler; Tom Twaddell, gardner; Isabell,			

	dairymaid; Nany Bell, undercooke; Pegg Tayler, chambermaid; Troth Stoker, chambermaid.) for year	5	8	0
Nov.	26.	(Annuities to sons Henry & Francis, £10 each)			
Dec.	2.	To the watchers of the leads for my neece Tempest safety	1	10	0
	4.	To Robin Wilson for worke horse shoeing	1	13	3
	13.	To John Chattoe for 28 yards of girth webb by Roger Maine	0	4	8
	21.	To Fenwick tayler for makeing the pypers' livery coate	0	4	0
	27.	To Cudy Reed for coles for burning lime in '99	7	0	0

1699/1700.

Jan.	6.	To my wife for a Neu Year's gift to her goddaughter Reed	0	5	0
	8.	To Cudy Brady of Barwick for 24 quarts of clarett wine by Robert Simmons	1	0	0
	16.	To Doctor Hume in handicaping Pott for his baye gelding 3 ginnies	3	4	6
	22.	To cosen Jack Clavering for all kinds of coales in '99 both for lime and house	22	5	0
		To the 2 quarters Barwick house sess payd by Robin Simmons Coachman	0	9	0
	30.	To Roger Maine a year's wage due Martinmass '99	5	0	0
		To Robert Simmons Coachman for a year's wage due last Michellmass	5	0	0
		To his son William Simmons for a year's wage due last Michellmass	2	10	0
Feb.	6.	To Mr. Glover for painting neece Tempest clossett with wainscott culler	1	9	0
	9.	To my wife for charges att Bitchwood[89] Mrs. Grey's crissening	0	10	6

[89] Bitchwood, now Birchwood, in Eglingham parish, the patrimony of the Greys of Kyloe. Mrs. Grey was Frances, daughter of Francis Brandling of Hoppen. She married Bryan Grey on 12 October, 1696. The child christened was probably Elizabeth, who married in 1724 Thomas Grey of Morton. (Information from Mr. Charles Gray of Donohill, Tipperary.)

		To Willy Smith for draweing my godsonn Tom Howard anuity and counterpart	0	5	0
Feb.	10.	Lent Robin Attkin maisson in part of wage for worke	2	0	0
		For damask for 4 table cloaths and 2 dosen napkins by cosen Fleetwood	6	8	6
	15.	To (Willy Smith *erased*) my godsonn Tom Howard given	1	0	0
		To Adam Lamb for his quarter's rent due Kandellmass '99	1	5	0
		To the two sisters Mrs. Mary Thornton and Mrs. Helen Widdrington for the intrest of £1050 due last January by sonn Ned and payd by me[90]	31	10	0
	17.	To sonn Ned to cleer as by his acquittance Hazellrigg Kandellmass rent for 99; without any alloweances: but all in ready monie	60	0	0
	21.	To Francis Tomson collectour; two last quarters' taxes for Fenwick and Buckton land tyeth sess for 99 by his acquittance	11	12	5
	23.	To Willy Frizell for 40 quarts sack att 13d per quart; by cosen Fleetwood	2	3	4
	26.	To George Clark lowlick carryer for goods brought my wife 26 stone by cosen Fleetwood	0	13	0
	28.	To Coll Hyde in charity by my wife	1	0	0
		To sonn Harry for a sadle bridle and furnitur	3	9	0
	29.	To Tho: murton collector for 4 quarters' sess for Coldburne in 99 by Roger maine	2	1	7
March	5.	For dringking glasses and a possett glass by cosen Fleetwood	0	8	6

1699/1700.

	5.	To mad cosen Mary Haggerston in charity	0	5	0

---

[90] See Introduction, p. xiii.

To Mathew Sibbett of Longe Dyke Hall
collector for the land taxe for Ancroft
chappelry for year 99 for the two last
quarterly payments   13 18 8

To Rayph Watson of Fenham collector
for Holly Island chapellry for the land
taxe for the year 99 and for the two last
quarters' payment   2 5 10

March 12. To Will Chattoe marchant in Wooller to
cleer all in his books by cosen Fleetwood
from the begining of the world to this
day the 12 of this March   16 15 0

To Mathew Lintell for 2 paire of waine in-
shod wheels by Willy smith   2 18 0

13. To John Chatto for 26 spangle yarne att
2s. 5d. pr spangle   3 2 10

To John Chatto for 19 yards Holland att 4s.
pr yard   3 16 0

To John Chatto for 20 yards of muriss linin
cloath att 1s. 10d. pr yard   1 16 8

15. For 4 dosen bottles of clarett att Coldstream
att 14d per bottle by Anty peacock   2 16 0

18. To Sir William and Lady van Colster for
the purchase of Braxton for land and
corne tyeth—£1500 charges of stampt
paper parchment and draweing the writ-
tings—5.3.2 for 4 bonds—0.10.0 Mr. All-
good coming to Ryle and seeing all
executed—1.3.6 to councelor Lambton
3.10.6 To my Lady van Colster att pass-
ing the fine £12 charges of the fine pass-
ing all corts above and the examplication
£15 In all   1537 5 2
                                                        [sic]

My charges to Great Ryle att the execution
of Branxton purchase 15s. and the se-
curitys of renchargs out of Monilawes
for £135 haveing a rent charge of £665
with areers of rents before being £800
In all[91]   800 15 6

91 See Introduction, p. xiii.

March	20.	To Stobs Fenham for four sock molds and some steell by Willy Smith	o	8	8
		To Nany Cressy for wage; by cosen Fleetwood	1	5	o
		To Nany Cressy for the house use; by cosen Fleetwood	9	15	o
	24.	To Mrs. Ord of Weetwood for a valentine gift at Neucastle	2	15	o

1700.

	25.	To Doctor Hume by my wife a leue doare [*louis d'or*]	o	17	o
		To Mr. Sleigh by wife for bleeding her	o	5	o
	26.	To Mr. Patrick Smith and Mr. Cooper for serving the 5 chappelries	25	o	o
Apr.	1.	To my wife sent by her to Mrs. Selby's midwife and keeper	o	10	o
		To my wife for vallantine gift of Mance Reed	o	10	o
May	17.	To Davison, webster, for 38 yards linin cloath weaving	o	14	6
		To cosen Peggy Clavering for Hungary water for my wife by cosen Fleetwood	o	2	10
	19.	To Mr. Walter Ashley for a riding coates bob wigg	o	11	o
	31.	To Peter Potts upon Sir Francis Blake's acount and by his order out of Lowick Martinmass rents '99 for a larvoe charges	50	o	o
		To Sir Francis Blake for Lowick 1799 whittsonday rent and £5 arrear for last mart. which was allowed for 2 last quarters' sessess with 0.13.9 more So payd him in all for the last 2 halfe years rents with £5.13.9 for sessess In all	60	o	o
June	2.	To Mr. Bilton for makeing my gold scoope by Albert Silvertopp[92]	10	o	o
		To sonn Hary annuity by cosen Fleetwood	10	o	o
	4.	To sonn John for his anuity by Roger Maine	10	o	o

[92] Son of William Silvertop of Stella. Will dated 1736, proved 1738/9.

		To my wife to cleer Mr. Brandling's shop booke debt £57 and returned more for her use to London to Mrs. Eliza Thorold In all	100	0	0
		To my wife returned for London by Allbert Silvertopp	20	0	0
June	5.	To the Customer that seased of the salt in Holy Island by Hary Robison	2	0	0
	15.	To a Felton turner for 13 large milk bowles and 12 small dish bowles	0	18	0
	27.	To sonn Francis for his anuity Whittsonday 1700 by cosen Fleetwood	10	0	0
	30.	To Fenwick and Buckton pease carryers to Mr. Tom Grieves ship att Fenham being 600 bols pease by Tom Robison	0	13	3
July	4.	To my wife for a flowered night raile and aperon of musland	1	1	6
	16.	To charges riding post to honest William Archbould buriall at Annick[93]	0	16	0
	26.	To Captain Rober Midfor in charity as a condemned prisoner by my wife	1	0	0
		To sonn Ned for haire gold locketts made att London	4	10	0
		To sonn Ned for overpaying for pictors frames	0	12	0
Aug.	3.	To old Adam Smith for £100 intrest due 22 July last	3	0	0
	5.	To Mrs. Trumbull for 3 neu fashioned crevatts by Jemmy Crawford	5	4	0
		To Mr. Brandling for 2 boxes of sealing weafers and 12 light shaveing washballs	0	5	0
	8.	To John Chattoe for 3 paire washt leather rideing gloves	0	2	6
	15.	To Moyses tayler for makeing stayes for my wife by cosen Fleetwood	0	8	0
	25.	To Jemmy Crawford for plaine gold ring bought by my son Ned	9	14	9
	29.	To Mr. Ogle for a hagg oxe of his mother Selby's	3	17	0

[93] Died 14 July, 1700 (N.C.H.N. VII, 373).

			£	s	d
Aug.	30.	To Bewick millston winner for two mill stons for Lowick mill	2	8	0
Sept.	2.	To Mrs. Ord of Felkington nurse and mid-wife	0	10	0
	4.	To my wife for holland to make an allb	0	18	0
	13.	To Cudy Reed for 10 oxen att Whittingham faire £37 for Toule and charges 3s. 3d. in all	37	3	3
Oct.	10.	To Cheswick Gardner for 30 scoare of apels att 18s. pr six scoare by cosen Fleetwood	0	7	6
	13.	To Mr. Anton Counter of Barwick for two barrell of tarre by Jemmy Hann	1	12	0
Nov.	10.	To Coll. Robert Widdrington in charity by my wife a Leuy (*Louis*)	0	17	6
	15.	For charges with Lady Widdrington to Callalee[94]	2	0	0
		For takeing my horse att Hetton and finding my pistoll	0	3	6
	18.	(annuities to sons Harry & Francis £10 each) by cosen Fleetwood	20	0	0
	20.	To my grandson Francis pention by his uncle Will	10	0	0
Dec.	1.	To youngest Frank Haggerston for his anuety last martinmass by sonn Will[95]	10	0	0
		To sonn John for his anuety due last martinmass	10	0	0
	24.	My charges to Bidleston to see Tomye Selbye upon his coming home	0	14	0
		To sonn Hary for cards by cosen Fleetwood	0	3	6
1700/1.					
Jan.	1.	To Neu Year's gifts by my wife and selfe	25	1	3
		To Berrington sarvants when wee all dined there	2	5	0

[94] Jane Tempest, now married to Lord Widdrington; marriage bond, 15 April, 1700.

[95] Francis Haggerston junior would now be entering the Benedictine novitiate at Douai. The "pension" would be his grandfather's contribution towards his keep there, the "annuity" a personal allowance pending his reaching the age of 21. After the settlement of 1702 (see introduction p. xi), William Haggerston would be responsible for payment.

	To Mr. Lance Allgood atturney for Branxton post fine payd by Allb. Silvertopp	3	15	0
	To Mr. John Crawford vicker of Branxton in full of his quarter stypend due last Martinmass	5	0	0
Jan. 24.	To Jemmy Crawford for wormwood water att Durham for my wife by cosen Fleetwood	0	4	6
27.	To Betty Maine for fourteen yards of Huckaback for napkins by cosen Fleetwood	0	14	0
Feb. 6.	by my order to Mr. Francis Brandling to pay Lady Charleton for my sonn John's anuety due last martinmass 1700	10	0	0
	To Roger Maine a year's wage due Candlemas	5	0	0
	To Robert Simmons half year's wage	2	10	0
	To Robert Simmons for his son Willys year's wage due martinmass	2	10	0
March 1.	To Doctour Hume when sonn Frank was sick[96]	1	0	0
	To Hary Slight for bleeding him then[97]	0	10	0

1701.

	To Mr. Smith in Edenburge monument maker 10 dollers	2	5	0
Apr. 14.	To Nelly Steell the nurse by my wife 2 dollers	0	9	0
May 3.	To cosen Mary Thornton and cosen Widdrington for their £1050 halfe year's intrest due from sonn Ned last Kandellmass 1700	31	10	0
11.	To Cudy Reed for Budle cockles before and in last lent	1	12	0
	To Mr. John Sleight for bleeding my wife	0	5	0

---

[96] First mention of his last illness.
[97] Henry Sleight of Berwick, apothecary, married Mary Watson of Goswick (R.N.D. 186).

May	21.	To charges att Barwick for 87 bols bigg and 80 bols wheat Wooller measure	1	7	9
	25.	To Robison to cleer the two last shipp loading of bigg and wheat carrages	1	8	5
	28.	For two sammon for the house use	0	2	6
June	2.	My charges to Bidleston about Potts land in Farnham	0	13	0
	4.	To my cosen Peggy Clavering for a primmer	0	5	6
		For a brass paire of sniffers with boxe to stand on	0	2	6
		To charges att Bellford in cosen Clavering's journey	0	9	0
	11.	To sonn Hary for his anuity now due by cosen Fleetwood	10	0	0
		To sonn Francis for his halfe years anuity now due by cosen Fleetwood	10	0	0
		To grandson Frank for his halfe year's pention now due by his uncull Will	10	0	0
July	10.	To Bengy Grieve for a treat of sweett-meats and wine for cosen Rayph Lambton lady and her sister Hedworth[98] by cosen Fleetwood	1	8	0
	15.	To charges at Bidleston and Ellingham with my wife	2	12	0
	15.	To cosen Mary Thornton and her sister £1050 intrest due 9 July and payd at Witton Shields	31	10	0
	18.	To sonn Jacky for his anuity due last Whittsonday payd Lady Charleton for his use upon my order to mr. Francis Brandling marchant in Neucastle	10	0	0
Aug.	13.	To Capt. Robert Midford in charity by my wife	1	0	0
	14.	To Robert Jemmison for Ancroft church sirplice	0	10	0

[98] Ralph Lambton's wife was Dorothy, daughter of John Hedworth of Harraton and Anne James of Washington. Her sister would be Elizabeth Hedworth, later (1703) married to Sir William Williamson Bart. of Monkwearmouth.

Sept.	3.	Charges att Neucastle with Mr. Fardinando Forster's corpes in waiting the . . . to Bambrough[99]	0	16	6
Oct.	27.	To Roger Maine for a filly foale	1	0	0
Nov.	9.	To Tom Beadnell for a vyolinn by cosen Fleetwood	0	15	0
	12.	To Mr. Thomas Orde of Felkington for Farnam potts rent due last martinmass	3	0	0
		To sonn Hary for his 1701 martinmas anuity by cosen Fleetwood	10	0	0
		To sonn Francis for his 1701 martinmas anuity by cosen Fleetwood	10	0	0
	24.	To cosen Peggy Clavering for a Topping for my wife[100]	0	5	6
Dec.	26.	To Doctor Hume for visiting my wife	1	1	6

1701/2.

Jan.	14.	To Tom Smith my Godson for a Neu Year's gift	0	5	0
Feb.	2.	To cosen Fleetwood for sallary now due	7	10	0
	4.	To sonn Francis for doctors and phisick in his sickness by cosen Fleetwood	11	8	0
	5.	To Roger Maine a year's wage	5	0	0
	12.	To cosen Fleetwood for Spittle Tinker mending the brueing copper and panns	0	4	0
	25.	To Robert Simmons a year's wage due Michellmass 1701	6	0	0
		To Robert Simmons servants for all harvest wage	1	3	11
	26.	Mrs. Mary Thornton and Helen Widdrington by Roger Maine	28	15	0
March	2.	To George Smith cleering all taxes of Royal rent due last Martinmas 1701	14	10	1
		To George Smith Baylieff cleering charges of Cort dinners to Martinmass 1701	8	10	0
		To George Smith Baylieff cleering his 2 years sallary to Martinmass 1701	13	6	8

[99] Son of Sir William Forster of Bamburgh and Dorothy Selby of Twisell, murdered in Newcastle by John Fenwick of Rock, 22 August, 1701.

[100] The topping or top-knot was the bow surmounting the headdress.

March 19.	To Berrington Gardner for twice bringing piedgons	0	2	0

1702.

Apr. 2. To Hary Robison for a neu coable makeing in Island ... 2 3 6

6. Lent old Robin Wilson smith in Fenwick by Willy Smith ... 2 0 0

12. To Mr. Wm. Chatto for a second murning sute and things for my wife by cosen Fleetwood ... 7 9 6

17. To young Mr. Luke Collingwood of Lanton in charity a ginny[101] ... 1 1 6

30. To Mr. Carmichell in generosity for giveing him the Holly Island cure and being baukett of it by an act of parliment by the Bishop[102] ... 5 0 0

May 14. To Brockmill weding for my wife and selfe by cosen Fleetwood ... 0 10 0

22. To Robin Attkins for building and pulling downe and pointing Branxton tower ... 8 0 0

24. ...Sonn Hary anuity by cosen Fleetwood ... 10 0 0
...Sonn Francis anuity by cosen Fleetwood ... 10 0 0
...Grandson Francis anuity by sonn Will ... 10 0 0

26. To Nelly Steell Mally's nurse by my wife ... 0 5 0
To Mr. Tho: Ord of Felkington for Farnham potts rent due Whittsonday last ... 3 0 0

June 4. To George Smith of Berrington weding by mance Reed ... 0 10 0

23. To Widdrington jorney with my wife and selfe ... 5 0 0

26. To Mr. Mayers two sarjants of Barwick for his giveing two marble pillars for my house there ... 0 10 0

July 2. My charges and wife's at Bidleston; coming and goeing ... 3 5 0

---

[101] Son of Luke Collingwood (d.1676), and grandson of Luke Collingwood (d.1708) and his wife Margaret Ramsay of Bewick.
[102] Lord Crewe.

July	3.	To Doctor Hume for John Murtons worke att my House in Barwick; and to the maison for setting up the two pillars att the doore	5	15	0
		To Doctor Hume for all other worke at Barwick House	13	18	0
	13.	To Alice Carnaby for stuff for a gowen 21 yards	1	1	0
	14.	To Robin Coachman for mending the Coach by cosen Fleetwood	0	1	0
	25.	To Capn Midford condemnd; in charity by my wife	1	0	0
	26.	To cosen Fill: Buttlers[103] wife; given a white paceing Galloway	4	0	0
	28.	To Bayliff John Pigg for two year's Bulimer house rent and sprigg with singletons due last martinmass to Barwick farmers of those rents	0	10	0
Aug.	5.	To cosen Fleetwood for sallary now due	7	10	0
		My charges to Bidleston and returne	0	17	0
	12.	To Rayph Heath maison for 12 scoare marble flaggs	1	10	0
	17.	To young lady Widdring. for sonn Jacks pention due Whittsonday last	10	0	0
	19.	To sonn Hary for four bookes	2	4	0
Sept.	10.	For 2 paire of draught oxen att Harbottle oxen faire	15	17	6
	15.	To London returnd for Frank Haggerston Whittsonday 1702 pention	10	0	0
		To Rayph Haggerston and cosen Margarys in charity	10	0	0
		To Mrs. Thorold for coach wheels three bed quilts Doctor Wilson and Doctor warrans mouth water; two kings speaches with charges	10	0	0
Oct.	9.	From Captain Collines and Lieutenant Rage for millkhouse grass for 120 Dragoon horses	131	16	6

[103] Brother of Fleetwood Butler.

Oct.	12.	To cosen Peggy Clavering for the red powder makeing for my wife	0	4	7
	16.	To Midleton and Fowbury groomes by my wife with her coach there	0	2	0
	25.	For coales for all uses for Haggerston 1702 from Shooeswood belonging to cosen Will Clavering 1180 bols payd	10	19	5
	30.	To the glass windowe sess for the yeare 1701	0	10	0
		For 3 dozen and halfe of brass plate bottons att Barwick	0	3	6
Nov.	4.	To Tom Batterton for bleeding my wife	0	5	0
	4.	To Docktour Hume for advice to my wife	0	10	0
	11.	To Bidleston charges with myselfe and servants	0	12	0
	16.	. . . Son Hary annuity by cosen Fleetwood	10	0	0
		. . . Son Francis annuity by cosen Fleetwood	10	0	0
		. . . Son Jacky annuity by Widdrington Buttler sent	10	0	0
	21.	To Docktour Hume for worke done at Haggerston House in Barwick	21	9	0
	28.	To Frank Haggerston younger's Anuity due payd daughter Haggerston by Willy Smith	10	0	0
Dec.	9.	To cosen Gifford[104] for a milk cowe 3 ginies	3	4	6
	21.	To Fish Tayler for makeing my cloath of gold waistcoate	0	4	6
	24.	To Crosby Barwick shoemaker for a paire of slippers by cosen Fleetwood	0	4	6
	29.	To Berington sarvants when my wife selfe sonns and daughters and grandsonns dyned there by cosen Fleetwood	1	2	6
		To Hary Sheperd's wife in charity	0	2	6

[104] See n.82.

1702/3.

Jan. 2. For costs of Hary Sheperd suite and releas-
ing him by Willy Smith with charges
and Baylieffs fees upon execution   13 10 0
To Hary Sheperd's wife in charity 2s. 6d.
and for one working for him In all   0 5 0

23. To Captain Wood in charity by my wife   1 0 0
To Fish Tayler for makeing a horse body
cloath; a paire of stockins for mad cosen
Mary; a paire of drawers for myselfe;
by cosen Fleetwood   0 2 6
To Tom Grieve for drugs for my wife by
cosen Fleetwood   0 15 0

25. To charges by my wife then att Barwick
by cosen Fleetwood   0 2 0

31. To Mary Ivisson for helping to make waxe
candells   0 1 0

Feb. 2. To Roger Maine for one year's wage due
last Michellmass   5 0 0

7. To sonn Ned to cleer a year's Rent for
Hasellrigg ending 2 Feb. last   120 0 0
To sonn Ned for Farnham year's Rent
due 11 Nov. 1702[105]   7 0 0

8. To James Mistris Ords coachman of Weetwood for carrying my wife and
daughters when her Coach broake from
Fenwick to Buckton; with their charges   0 9 0

10. To Robin Simmons one year's wage due
29 Sept. 1702   4 16 0
To cosen Fleetwood for tobaco and ale att
old Rayph Browens Buriall   0 7 6
To old George Davison for old Rayph
Browen's Buriall acording to Lawe[106]   0 2 0

19. To my godson Mr. Tho: Howard for a
year's anuity due 8 February 1702   21 0 0

[105] Hazelrigg valued at £120 a year and a rent charge of £7 a year out of Mark Potts' lands in Farnham, were included in the marriage settlement of Edward Haggerston in 1693.
[106] See entry for 30 September, 1691. Ralph Brown of Witton Shields, tailor, occurs in several lists of Papists, 1678-83.

March 1. To cosen Fleetwood for cloath for stocks
              and needles of James Hardy   0   4   6
         12. Lost at Fowbury att Leu 20 shillings with
              other charges   1   3   0
         21. To Doctor Hume for bleeding my wife   0 10   0

1703.
Apr.   4. To sonn William for his nephew Frank
              Whittsonday's Anuity for 1703 by
              mance Reed   10   0   0
         8. To Robin coachman when with my
             daughter Mrs. Bett Ord the two ladys of
             Berrington the horse charges at Barwick   0   1   6
        22. To charges att Goswick 4s. To Mick
             Pemerton in charity 3s. In all   0   7   0
             To my four grandchilder att severall times   1   0   0
        29. At Fowbury; three times playing att Leu   3   0   0
             To Felkington wedding for my wife and
             selfe by Anty Peacock   0 10   0
May   5. Lost at Buckton horse course   1 15   0
         7. For 200 oysters bought att the doore   0   7   0
        16. . . . Sonn Hary annuity by cosen Fleet-
             wood   10   0   0
             . . . Sonn Francis annuity by Willy
             Smith   10   0   0
        18. To cosen Fleetwood for cambrick for an
             allb   1   3   9
        22. To my brother Salvin repayd for Mr.
             Houseman two pictur of my brother
             and sister Blundells[107] given to neece
             Bridgett Garard[108]   4   0   0
        24. . . . Sonn Jacky annuity by Jack Dixson   10   0   0
             Given to Carnaby Jenny and little Nany   0   7   6
        27. To George Penny collectors for 1702
             windowe sess and John Sibbett   0 10   0

---

[107] William Blundell of Crosby, Lancs. and his wife Anne Haggerston, sister of
Sir Thomas.
[108] The first wife of Sir Francis Howard of Corby, brother-in-law of Sir Thomas
Haggerston, was a Gerard.

May	30.	To Tom Richardson for a prison sess for all my land in Lowick	0	6	4
June	10.	To Cosen Peggy Clavering in charity to buy a poore old man a cowe	0	10	0
	11.	To my Mall Haggerston a Fann and two paire of scocks	0	3	0
	19.	To sonn Francis for 3 allter cardes	0	5	0
July	2.	To Mr. Circkle watchmaker for a gold watch for my selfe	35	0	0
		To Mr. Circkle for a gold watch for my wife	22	0	0
	13.	To cosen Mary Thornton and Cosen Widdrington by cosen Fleetwood	28	15	0
	24.	To Fish Tayler for makeing my three Liveries and two shirrieff Liveries	2	2	0
	25.	To Willy Steell for Hazellrigg part for a neu joale building	0	19	8
	26.	To Robin Simmons for twice being with my wife and coach at Barwick	0	3	0
	30.	To Tom Beadnall for carage of my sillver stirrops; bosses; spurrs to a Branxton carryer	0	2	9
Aug.	9.	To Tom Forster's wife of Lowick for hay bought for the oxen by Tom Robison	0	10	0
	10.	To mad cosen Mary Haggerston's dyett with Troath Fish	3	12	0
		To all charges att her funerall and buriall in holy Island and for cakes, bread, alle brandy sack, tobaco, pypes, and wine £6.11.0. In all	7	0	0
	11.	To Haggerston, Fenwick, Buckton churchwardens att Bambrough when the Bishop was there present	0	8	0
Sept.	6.	To Sir William van Colster of Great Ryle barronett for finding a malicia horse for Lowick, Branxton and Langleyford ending at next Michellmass next coming 1703	15	0	0
	11.	To Robin Coachman for his sonn and Kitt's charges at Neucastle sizes	1	3	0

Sept.	17.	To John and Tom Scrowder for making the stone worke of the Gates	5	3	6
		theire dyett and lodgeing	1	12	0
	20.	To Mr. John Glen and his two men for wainscotting the red chamber	7	3	8
	29.	To John Short and Tom Steell for 1702 land taxe paid by Willy Smith	41	2	0
		To John Short and Tom Steell for mine and my wife poore sess	0	15	0
Oct.	1.	To Couldburn heard for two quarters' land taxe in 1703 for Couldburne	0	18	9
	13.	To John de Baptist for michellmass halfe years boate tyeth by Willy Smith	1	0	0
	27.	To Mrs. Thorold for chest of drawers, chaires, and stools 12; Table and looking glass with fraught to Barwick	22	0	0
		Returned to Mrs. Thorold to London by Allbert Silvertop	40	0	0
Nov.	4.	To cosen Fleetwood for a brass keckell	0	2	6
	11.	My charges to Bidlesston and back 11s. coach mending			
	14.	sonns Hary John and Francis by cosen Fleetwood and Willy Smith	30	0	0
	20.	To Doctor Hume for bleeding my wife a Luey [Louis]	0	17	6
	22.	To Captain Thomas Swinhoe in charity by my wife 1 ginny	1	1	6
	24.	To Mr. Circle for my wife's watch chaine by cosen Fleetwood	2	3	0
	28.	To cosen Will Clavering for all kinds of coales in 1703	24	13	2
	29.	To Edy Cook for Lowick Cort dinner	0	17	8
Dec.	9.	To Eslington Gardner for 12 Frutrees	0	15	0
		To charges for old Beadnell's buriell	2	15	0
	18.	To Tom Robison to cleer all charges of husbandry worke from martinmass 1702 for Fenwick and Buckton to martinmass 1703	127	1	0
		Att martinmass 1702 the sheep acount was 67 score and one od sheep, now att this			

	martinmass 1703 sheep acount—65 score and ten od sheep			
Dec. 26.	To the Haggerston inhabitants for all kind of husbandry worke from martinmass 1702 by Willy Smith	88	10	0

1703/4.

Jan. 14.	For eight yards of Cambrick for hand-corchers by cosen Fleetwood	1	1	0
27.	Lent Mr. Tho: Grey of Murton on a three years' bargin £40 to be payd halfe yearly	100	0	0
Feb. 10.	To Mr. Forster's groome when I dined att Ederston[109]	0	2	6
13.	To William Unthank of Ellyhaugh for four dozen of oxe bowes	1	4	0
15.	To widdow Mary Simmons a year's intrest due 2 last February	4	16	0
	To widdow Mary Simmons a year's wage due to her dead husband 29 last 7br.	6	0	0
	To Mary widdowe Simmons cleered all harvest worke due to her maide	0	16	4
	Roger Maine for a yer's wage due last michellmass	5	0	0
15.	To Roger Maine for £60 year's intrest due last February	3	12	0
	To Roger Maine for all harvest worke in 1703	1	4	0
29.	To the nurse and midwife att Felkington by my wife	0	10	0
	To Ned Scott for cureing my scabd horses in Lowick	0	6	0
March 5.	To Mrs. Parke[110] by my wife's order for the house use	3	0	0
	To cosen Fleetwood by my wife's order for the house use	1	11	0

---

[109] Thomas Forster (1659-1725); father of the Jacobite general.

[110] Daughter of Gilbert Parke of Warton, later housekeeper with the Salvins at Croxdale, where she died in 1734 (Salvin MSS.).

March	6.	To my four Grandchilder four halfe Crowens and 2s. in brass In all	0	12	0
	7.	To Coll. Hyde in charity by my wife	1	0	0
	10.	To sonn Francis to beare charges in his sickness in Barwick	10	0	0
	18.	To Tomas Tomson for four quarters' payment of sess for Coldburne in 1703	1	17	6
		for bridge sess for Coldburne in 1703	0	0	11

1704.

	28.	To Mathew Bell's sonn for all Lowick land in my hands for the last quarters sess for 1703	1	17	6
Apr.	13.	To Widdow Reed for £300 year's intrest by Tom Robison due 25 March last	15	0	0
	20.	To Mr. Chattoe for all kind of murning for sonn Francis by cosen Fleetwood	36	0	0
		To Mr. Luke Collingwood for five bookes	1	10	0
		To Mr. Luke Collingwood in charity att Easter	1	0	0
	20.	To sonn Francis funerall charges all maner of ways[111]	145	15	9
May	27.	To my wife's charge att Bidleston in visetting neece Selby indisposed	1	7	6
June	2.	To cosen Fleetwood for 6 bottles of cidar from Neucastle	0	6	0
	9.	Sons Hary and Jacky 1704 salary by cosen Fleetwood	20	0	0
	14.	To my four grandchielder to buy fairings at Barwick	0	10	0
	20.	To Nelly Dannise's wedding at Berrington for my wife and selfe by Mrs. Parke	0	10	0
July	8.	To Widdrington charges my wife and selfe	3	0	0
		My wife's and my charges at Chillingham[112] and Eatall	0	5	0

---

[111] See Introduction, p. xi.

[112] Charles Bennet, later Earl of Tankerville and his wife Mary, last of the Grey of Chillingham.

July	15.	To Willy Steell for a gold cross set with crisstall	3	0	0
	22.	To Fish for a suite of second murning makeing and soweing drawing roome hangings	0	13	6
	27.	To Mr. Fish for painting the wainscott roome being 123 feet att 12d, per foot	6	13	2
Aug.	1.	Given by wife to cosen Mary Craine[113] her goddaughter a 5 ginny peece which when gold went att the heigh cost me	7	10	0
		For a top knott for little Mally given by wife	0	2	6
	6.	To Captain Midford in charity by little Mally Haggerston	0	10	0
	24.	To Tomy Smith my Godson of Hillhead	0	2	6
Oct.	7.	To Doctour Cooper for fees by cosen Fleetwood	2	0	0
		To Doctour Strather for fees 5 ginies by cosen Fleetwood[114]	5	7	6
		To Doctour Hume for fees by cosen Fleetwood	3	0	0
Nov.	2.	To cosen Fleetwood for four dozen quinces	0	4	0
	8.	To Coll. Hyde in charity by my wife	1	0	0
		To Coll. Hyde in charity to other poor soules	1	0	0
	19.	To sonn Hary for Martinmas stypend 1704 by cosen Fleetwood	10	0	0
		To sonn John for Martinmass sallary 1704 by cosen Fleetwood	10	0	0
Dec.	3.	To cosen Fleetwood for whipcord for draweing curtains up	0	2	6
	6.	To John Maine for hyere as a fisherman by John Pawliner	0	2	6
	8.	To cosen Fleetwood for old Rayph Beadnall's buriall	0	4	0

[113] Daughter of Francis Crane of Woodrising, Norfolk, and his wife Mary Widdrington. The price of the guinea reached thirty shillings sterling about June, 1695. (A. Feaveryear, *The Pound Sterling*, p. 131.)

[114] Probably Edward Strother, M.D.; practised successively in Alnwick, Newcastle and London; died in his house in Soho, 13 April, 1737; married Mary Morrison of Eslington (Whittingham reg.), 15 January, 1697/8.

1704/5.

Jan.	9.	To my neece Jarrett a ginny[115]	1	1	6
	19.	To Carnaby Haggerston given	0	5	0
Feb.	4.	To John Walker buttler for a years wage by cosen Fleetwood	4	0	0
	5.	To Mary Simmons for £80 intrest now due	4	16	0
	21.	To Coll. Hyde of Ashweddensday in charity by my wife	1	0	0

1705.

Apr.	8.	To cosen Fleetwood for holland for an Allb	1	19	8
	10.	To Jemmy Crawford for green silck for my wife at Annick faire	0	3	0
	28.	To the nurse and midwife at Widdring. by Mance Reed two ginnies[116]	2	4	6
May	17.	To Cornelius for coach harness mending £0.2.6; for 6 halters 18d.; Charges at Barwick with nephew and neece Hodshon 0.2.0[117] In all	0	6	0
June	11.	Sonn Hary annuity by cosen Fleetwood	10	0	0
	14.	To Mr. Anderton in charity by my wife[118]	0	10	0
	18.	Sonn John annuity by cosen Fleetwood	10	0	0
July	2.	To William, Widdrington buttler, for five months wage here by my wife	2	10	0
	3.	To my Godson Frank Ashley in charity	0	2	6
	29.	To Mary Thornton and her sister Widdrington	28	15	0
Aug.	23.	To Mr. Fennick watchmaker for worke done	0	5	0
Sept.	6.	To my neece Hodgson's midwife and nurse by sonn Ned 2 ginies	2	3	0

---

[115] See n.108.

[116] Alethea Widdrington, aged 14 in 1719.

[117] Philip Hodgson was the son of Mary Haggerston, sister of Sir Thomas, by her second husband, Lancelot Hodgson. His wife was Anne (or Mary) daughter of Allan Swinburne of Tone.

[118] Probably Francis Anderton, S.J. later chaplain at Haggerston.

Sept.	14.	To Michael Pemmerton in charity	0	5	0
Oct.	5.	To my wife for midwife and nurse att Eatall	0	10	0
Nov.	12.	(Sons Hary and Jacky annuities by cosen Fleetwood)	20	0	0
		To sonn Will for Frank Haggerston's pention by Willy Smith	10	0	0
		To sonn Will for Frank Haggerston anuity now due by Willy Smith	10	0	0

1705/6.

March	2.	To cosen Mary Thornton and Widdow Widdring. for halfe a year's intrest due last January upon sonn Neds acount	28	15	0
	19.	To cosen Fleetwood for staire case picture att Barwick	4	3	0

1706.

Apr.	10.	To Berrington fiddlers at Will. Clavering's wedding[119]	0	5	0
	22.	To my neece Betty Howard att parting given 5 ginnies	5	7	6
May	16.	Sonn Hary annuity by cosen Fleetwood	10	0	0
	10.	To my two granddaughters att parting for York by my wife and selfe[120]	2	3	0
June	12.	To sonn Will for Frank Haggerstons anuity	10	0	0
	12.	To sonn Will for cosen Margarey Haggerston use to be return	10	0	0
Aug.	1.	To cosen Fleetwood Buttler for sallary	7	10	0
	5.	To sonn John for his Anuity due last Whittsonday by cosen Fleetwood	10	0	0
	7.	To my two granddaughters att York by Mr. Mettim two halfe ginnies[121]	1	1	6
	10.	To cosen Bridgett Buttler returnd to London by Captain Savige	20	0	0

[119] William Clavering "married at Newsham by a popish priest" (Kyloe reg.) to Anne daughter of Edward Widdrington of Felton.

[120] The convent at York Bar and its sister house at Hammersmith were then the only convent schools in England.

[121] Probably Philip Sylvester Metham, O.S.B., then at York.

Sept.	12.	To Mr. Abell for museick five ginnies and his two men 20s. In all	6	7	6
	15.	To Johnson of Haughhead for a hogshead of clarett by Willy Steell	13	0	0
Nov.	26.	(Wages: Cornelius coachman £3; Robin Daye £1.5.0; Mance Reed £2.10.0; John Gibson, a year, £4; John Gardner £2; Cowherd £1.5; Robin Spence the swineboy 15s.; Mary Ivison cook £2; Nany Errington £1.5; Peggy Hann (3 qrtrs) £1.10; Nelly Wilson dairymaid £1; Betty Havery undercook 15s.)			
		Sons Hary and Jacky annuities	20	0	0
Dec.	19.	To sonn Ned for Frank Haggerston's martinmass annuity	10	0	0

1706/7.

Jan.	2.	To cosen Fleetwood for my wife att Berrington's sick wife	0	10	0
	22.	To my wife at Berrington midwife and nurse[122]	0	10	0
		To my daughter Ned [wife] for setting a Lock of heirre in	1	1	0
Feb.	2.	To Watt Ashley for a neu fashion wigg	2	0	0
	6.	To Mary Simmons for £20 intrest due to Robin her son	1	4	0
		To a shipwracked Lord's sonn by cosen Fleetwood	0	5	0
		To cosen Fleetwood for oranges and red herring	0	7	6
		To Tom Scrowder for alltering sonn Hary's chimney by cosen Fleetwood	1	0	0
March	10.	Cosen Mary Thornton and cosen Widd-rington Hasell. Kandellmass rent for 1706 upon sonn Ned's acount	28	15	0

1707.

May	9.	To Mrs. Armor late of Ellingham in charity by my wife a ginny	1	1	6

[122] The child would be William Clavering who died February, 1789, aged 82.

		To the danceing maister's musick by boe(?)	0	5	0
July	17.	My joyney and wifes to Widdrington	16	0	0
Aug.	23.	To sonn Will for my grandson Frank's anuity due last Whittsonday	10	0	0
		To cosen Bridgett Buttler for plate by sonn Will	8	6	6
Sept.	9.	Sons Hary and John's annuities due Whitsunday 1707	20	0	0
	19.	For a paire of London silver spurrs to sonn Ned	2	3	0
Oct.	17.	To sonn Will to get returnd to cosen Margery by cosen Fleetwood	7	10	0
Nov.	5.	To sonn Will for Frank Haggerston's anuity £7 and £3 for a fatt oxe In all	10	0	0
	21.	To Edy Cooke for the Cort dinner in 1707	1	1	0
Dec.	10.	To sonn Hary's anuity by cosen Fleetwood	10	0	0
		To cosen Bridgett to discharge cosen Margery Haggerston funerall	8	7	6
		To cosen Bridgett Buttler for travelling charges to Haggerston	5	7	6
	21.	To my wife in charity to cosen Forster Loneridge	1	1	6

1707/8.

Jan.	2.	In Neu Year's gifts	25	2	0
Feb.	6.	To my two cosens Thorntons upon sonn Ned's acount by Mr. Francis Brandling	28	15	0
	20.	To Coll. Hyde for sonn John's anuity due last martinmass	10	0	0
		To cosen Fleetwood for monie Peggy Paxton[123] layd out for my wife	0	5	6
May	13.	To the nurse att Berrington by my selfe[124]	0	5	0

1708.

June	2.	To old Will. Simm. in charity	0	5	0

[123] In service at Everingham (Sir Marmaduke Constable) in 1724 (Everingham MSS.).
[124] The birth of Edward Clavering, executed at York, 1 November, 1746, for his part in the Jacobite rising.

June	18.	To my sonn Hary for his Whittsonday anuity by cosen Fleetwood	10	0	0
		To sonn Jacky for his Whittsonday anuity by cosen Fleetwood	10	0	0
	18.	To Frank Dunn in charity being a prisoner	1	0	0
		To Fish for makeing five murning suites	2	0	0
		To Grace Cary for charges att deare sonn Will's goeing to Island	5	10	5
		To deare sonn Will's buriall att the Island by Willy Smith	1	10	0
	20.	To old Mr. Bryan Grey for 660 bols of coales	6	10	0
July	3.	To Cornelius Wilson upon Patrick Ripath's acount	3	10	0
	28.	For a veale cawlfe when Coll. Ratcliff was here to Jemy Hann[125]	0	8	6
	29.	To Lord Ossulton for a years rent for Hedon and Warks middle demain	25	0	0
Nov.	23.	(Sons Hary and John annuities)	20	0	0
		To Lord Widdrington for Mr. Wrighty's Plate	16	15	6
Dec.	2.	To two men and two women for drawing oyle from the monstir fish	0	9	0
		To cosen Bridgett Buttler for my wife by her sister	0	16	6
		To cosen Fleetwood for night railes for my wife	1	9	6
		To Will Chatto for a she ass for my wife	5	7	8
	17.	To the nurse at Widdrington by wife two ginnies	2	3	0

1708/9.

Feb.	10.	Payd for 200 morgage of Monielawes by Sr. William and Lady van Colster to Carnaby Haggerston	200	0	0

[125] Thomas, third son of Francis Radcliffe, first Earl of Derwentwater and Katherine Fenwick of Meldon; prisoner in the Tower of London October, 1678-May, 1680; colonel in the English army, commission in the Duke of Newcastle's Regt. of Foot, 29 September, 1688. Died unmarried at Douai, 31 December, 1715.

March 11.	To my cosen Bridgett for stocken and lace for my wife	0	14	0
19.	To Longeridge cosen Forster in charity by my wife	1	1	6
	To Longridge cosen Forster in charity by my wife three bols wheat	1	10	0
	To Frank Dunn's wife in charity by my wife	1	0	0

1709.

26.	To Tom Ord of Island for 1000 sprats by cosen Fleetwood	0	4	0
	To Tom Ord of Island for another 1000 sprats	0	4	0
	To sonn Jacky by my wife a ginnie	1	1	6
	To Barbara Buttler halfe a ginnie	0	10	9
May 5.	To Sir William van Colster for Monie-lawes purchase	1300	0	0
June 7.	For a neu coach seate for Cornelius by cosen Fleetwood	1	0	6
10.	To my daughter May Haggerston for an ass and foale 5 ginnies	5	7	6
30.	To sonn Hary for aneuity by cosen Fleetwood	10	0	0
July 4.	To a Barbacastle man for nine bridle two snafles nine tabbs	0	15	9
8.	To sonn Jacky and grandsonn Frank for their halfe year's anuitys due last Whitt-sonday by sonn Ned	20	0	0
12.	To Haggerston, Fenwick, and Buckton churchwardens when they were summoned to Neucastle to apeare by the Bishop	1	15	0
22.	To Barbara Buttler for course cloath for my wife	2	0	0
24.	To Crosby shoomaker for shoes for my wife and selfe	0	7	0
26.	To my wife given cosen Bridgett (last entry)	2	3	0

INDEX

SURTEES SOCIETY CONSTITUTION,
PUBLICATIONS AND LIST
OF MEMBERS.

SURTEES SOCIETY

ESTABLISHED IN THE YEAR 1834

In honour of the late Robert Surtees of Mainsforth, Esquire, the author of the History of the County Palatine of Durham, and in accordance with his pursuits and plans; having for its object the publication of inedited Manuscripts, illustrative of the intellectual, the moral, the religious, and the social condition of those parts of England and Scotland included on the east between the Humber and the Firth of Forth, and on the west between the Mersey and the Clyde, a region which constituted the ancient kingdom of Northumbria.

NEW RULES AGREED UPON IN 1849; REVISED 1863, 1925, 1954 AND 1967

I.—There shall be a Patron of the Society, who shall be President.

II.—There shall be up to twenty-four Vice-Presidents, and a Secretary, and Editor and a Treasurer.

III.—The Patron and President, the Vice-Presidents, the Secretary and the Treasurer shall form the Council, any five of whom, including the Secretary and the Treasurer, shall be a quorum competent to transact the business of the Society.

IV.—The Patron and President, the Vice-Presidents, the Secretary and the Treasurer shall be elected at the general meetings of the Society, as vacancies in such offices occur.

V.—Any vacancies in the office of Secretary or Treasurer shall be provisionally filled up by the Council, subject to the approbation of the next general meeting.

VI.—Two meetings of the Council shall be held in every year in the months of June and December, and the place and hour of meeting shall be fixed by the Council and communicated by the Secretary to the members of the Council.

VII.—The meeting in June shall be the Anniversary, and shall be open to any member of the Society.

VIII.—The Secretary shall convene extraordinary meetings of the Council on a requisition to that effect, signed by not less than five members of the Council, being presented to him.

IX.—Each member shall pay in advance to the Treasurer the annual sum of two guineas. If any member's subscription shall be in arrear for two years, and he shall neglect to pay his subscription after having been reminded by the Treasurer, he shall be regarded as having ceased to be a member of the Society.

X.—The money raised by the Society shall be expended in publishing such compositions, in their original language, or in a translated form, as come within the scope of this Society, without limitation of time with reference to the period of their respective authors. All editorial and other expenses to be defrayed by the Society.

XI.—One volume at least, in a closely printed octavo form, shall be supplied to each member of the Society every year, free of expense. Each annual subscription shall carry with it the right to one volume during that year, even if that is not the volume for the year. Members who have paid subscriptions for years for which no volume has yet been issued are entitled to all future publications, irrespective of the years for which they are issued, until such time as they shall have received a volume for every annual suscription paid.

XII.—If the funds of the Society in any year will permit, the Council shall be at liberty to print and furnish to the members, free of expense, any other volume or volumes of the same character, in the same or a different form.

XIII.—The number of copies of each publication, and the selection of a printer and publisher, shall be left to the Council, who shall also fix the price at which the copies not furnished to members shall be sold to the public.

XIV.—The armorial bearings of Mr. Surtees, and some other characteristic decoration connecting the Society with his name, shall be used in each publication.

XV.—A list of the officers and members, together with an account of the receipts and expenses of the Society, shall be made up every other year to the time of the annual meeting, and shall be submitted to the Society to be printed and published as the meeting shall direct.

XVI.—No alteration shall be made in these rules, except at an annual meeting. Notice of any such alteration shall be given at least as early as the ordinary meeting of the Council immediately preceding.

PUBLICATIONS OF THE SURTEES SOCIETY

† *Indicates that the volume is out of print.*
* *Indicates that copies can be supplied from back stock by the Society's agent Wm. Dawson & Son Ltd., Back Issues Department, Canon House, Folkestone, Kent, at a price of £2. 0. 0d to members (if orders are placed through the Society) and £2. 10. 0d. to non-members.*
r *Indicates that reprint copies can be supplied by the Society's agent Wm. Dawson & Son Ltd., Back Issues Department, Canon House, Folkestone, Kent, at a special price to members (if orders are placed through the Society).*

†1. Reginaldi Monachi Dunelmensis Libellus de Admirandis Beati Cuthberti Virtutibus. Edited by Dr. Raine.

r2. Wills and Inventories, illustrative of the History, Manners, Language, Statistics, etc., of the Northern Counties of England, from the Eleventh Century downwards. (Chiefly from the Registry of Durham). Vol. I. Edited by Dr. Raine. See vols. 38, 112, 142.

†3. The Towneley Mysteries, or Miracle Plays. Edited by J. Gordon. The Preface by Joseph Hunter.

†4. Testamenta Eboracensia: Wills, illustrative of the History, Manners, Language, Statistics, etc., of the Province of York, from 1300 downwards. Vol. I. Edited by Dr. Raine. See vols. 30, 45, 53, 79, 106.

†5. Sanctuarium Dunelmense et Sanctuarium Beverlacense; or, Registers of the Sanctuaries of Durham and Beverley. Edited by Dr. Raine. The Preface by the Rev. T. Chevalier.

†6. The Charters of Endowment, Inventories, and Account Rolls of the Priory of Finchale in the County of Durham. Edited by Dr. Raine.

†7. Catalogi Veteres Librorum Ecclesiae Cathedralis Dunelm.

Jarrow and Monkwearmouth, from their commencement in 1303 until the Dissolution. Edited by Dr. Raine.

†30. Testamenta Eboracensia: Wills illustrative of the History, Manners, Language, Statistics, etc., of the Province of York, from 1429 to 1467. Vol. II. Edited by the Rev. J. Raine. See vols. 4, 45, 53, 79, 106.

†31. The Bede Roll of John Burnaby, Prior of Durham (1456-1464). With illustrative documents. Edited by Dr. Raine.

r32. The Survey of the Palatinate of Durham, compiled during the Episcopate of Thomas Hatfield (1345-1382). Edited by the Rev. W. Greenwell.

†33. The Farming Book of Henry Best, of Elmswell in the East Riding of Yorkshire. Edited by the Rev. C. B. Norcliffe.

†34. The Proceedings of the High Court of Commission for Durham and Northumberland. Edited by W. H. D. Longstaffe.

†35. The Fabric Rolls of York Minster. Edited by the Rev. J. Raine.

†36. The Heraldic Visitation of Yorkshire by Sir William Dugdale in 1665. Edited by R. Davies.

†37. A volume of Miscellanea, comprising the Letters of Dean Granville, the Account of the Siege of Pontefract by Nathan Drake, and Extracts from the Rokeby Correspondence. Edited by the Rev. George Ornsby, W. H. D. Longstaffe and the Rev. J. Raine. See vols. 47, 127.

r38. A Volume of Wills from the Registry of Durham. Edited by the Rev. W. Greenwell. See vols. 2, 112, 142.

†39. The Gospel of St. Mark, from the Northumbrian Interlinear Gloss to the Gospels contained in the Cotton MS. Nero D.IV. Edited by G. Waring. See vols. 28, 43, 48.

†40. A selection from the Depositions in Criminal Cases taken before the Northern Magistrates; from the Originals preserved in York Castle. Saec.XVII. Edited by the Rev. J. Raine.

†41. The Heraldic Visitation of the North of England made in 1530 by Thomas Tonge. With an Appendix of Genealogical MSS. Edited by W. H. D. Longstaffe.

†42. Memorials of Fountain Abbey. Vol. I. Comprising the Chronicle relating to the Foundation of the House, written by Hugh de Kirkstall; the Chronicle of Abbats, etc., and an

Historical description of the Abbey, with Illustrations. Edited by J. R. Walbran. See vols. 67, 130.

†43. The Gospel of St. Luke, from the Northumbrian Interlinear Gloss to the Gospels contained in the Cotton MS. Nero D.IV. Edited by G. Waring. See vols. 28, 39, 48. 17s. 6d.

†44. The Priory of Hexham, its Chronicle, Endowments and Annals. Vol. I. Containing the Chronicles, etc., of John and Richard, Priors of Hexham, and Aelred, Abbat of Rievaulx, with an Appendix of Documents and a Preface illustrated with Engravings. Edited by the Rev. J. Raine. See vol. 46.

†45. Testamenta Eboracensia: Wills illustrative of the History, Manners, Language, Statistics, etc., of the Province of York, from 1467 to 1487. Vol. III. Edited by the Rev. J. Raine. See vols. 4, 30, 53, 79, 106. 21s.

†46. The Priory of Hexham. Vol. II. Containing the Liber Niger, with Charters and other Documents and a Preface illustrated with Engravings. Edited by the Rev. J. Raine.

†47. The Letters, etc., of Dennis Granville, D.D., Dean of Durham, from the Originals recently discovered in the Bodleian Library. Part II. Edited by the Rev. G. Ornsby. See vol. 37.

†48. The Gospel of St. John from the Northumbrian Interlinear Gloss to the Gospels in the Cotton MS. Nero D.IV. With Preface and Prolegomena. Edited by G. Waring. See vols. 28, 39, 43.

†49. The Survey of the County of York, taken by John de Kirkby, commonly called Kirkby's Inquest. Also Inquisitions of Knights' Fees, the Nomina Villarum for Yorkshire, and an Appendix of illustrative Documents. Edited by R. H. Scaife.

†50. Memoirs of the Life of Ambrose Barnes, Merchant and sometime Alderman of Newcastle upon Tyne. Edited by W. H. D. Longstaffe.

†51. Symeon of Durham. The whole of the Works ascribed to him, except the History of the Church of Durham. To which are added the History of the Translation of St. Cuthbert, the Life of St. Margaret, Queen of Scotland, by Turgot, Prior of Durham, etc. Edited by J. H. Hinde.

†52. The Correspondence of John Cosin, Bishop of Durham. Vol. I. Edited by the Rev. G. Ornsby. See vol. 55.

†53. Testamenta Eboracensia. Vol. IV. From 1485 to 1500. Edited by the Rev. J. Raine. See vols. 4, 30, 45, 79, 106.

†54. The Diary of Abraham De Lay Pryme, the Yorkshire Antiquary. Edited by C. Jackson.

†55. The Correspondence of John Cosin, Bishop of Durham. Vol. II. Edited by the Rev. G. Ornsby.

†56. The Register of Walter Gray, Archbishop of York, 1215-1255. Edited by the Rev. J. Raine.

†57. The Register of the Guild of Corpus Christi in the City of York, containing a Full List of its Members. Edited by R. H. Skaife.

†58. Feodarium Prioratus Dumelmensis: A Survey of the Estates of the Prior and Convent of Durham in the Fifteenth Century. Edited by the Rev. W. Greenwell.

†59. Missale ad usum insignis Ecclesiae Eboracensis. The York Missal. Vol. I. Edited by Henderson.

†60. The Same. Vol. II. By the same Editor.

†61. Liber Pontificalis Chr. Bainbridge Aechiepiscopi Eboracensis. The York Pontifical. Edited by Henderson.

†62. The Autobiography of Mrs. Alice Thornton, of East Newton, co. York. Saec. XVII. Edited by C. Jackson.

†63. Manuale et Processionale ad usum insignis Ecclesiae Eboracensis. The York Manual and Processional. Edited by Henderson.

†64. Acts of Chapter of the Collegiate Church of SS. Peter and Wilfrid, Ripon, 1452-1506. Edited by the Rev. J. T. Fowler.

†65. Yorkshire Diaries and Autobiographies in the Seventeenth and Eighteenth Centuries. Vol. I. Edited by C. Jackson. See vol. 77.

†66. Cartularium Abbatiae de Novo Monasterio (Newminster). Edited by the Rev. J. T. Fowler.

†67. Memorials of Fountains Abbey. Vol. II. Comprising the Royal Charters and some of the Papal Grants, etc. Edited by J. R. Walbran and the Rev. J. Raine. See vols. 42, 130.

†68. Selections from the Household Books of Lord William Howard, of Naworth Castle. Edited by the Rev. G. Ornsby.

†69. The Chartulary of Whitby. Vol. I. Edited by the Rev. J. C. Atkinson.

†70. A selection from the Poems of Lawrence, Prior of Durham. Saec. XII. Edited by the Rev. J. Raine.

†71. The York Breviary. Vol. I. Edited by the Hon. and Rev. S. Lawley.

†72. The Chartulary of Whitby. Vol. II. Edited by the Rev. J. C. Atkinson. See vol. 69.

†73. The Life and Correspondence of the Rev. William Stukeley, M.D., the Antiquary. Vol. I. Edited by the Rev. W. C. Lukis.

†74. Memorials of the Church of Ripon. Vol. I. Edited by the Rev. J. T. Fowler.

†75. The York Breviary. Vol. II. Edited by the Hon. and Rev. S. Lawley. See vol. 71.

†76. The Life and Correspondence of the Rev. William Stukeley. Vol. II. Edited by the Rev. W. C. Lukis. See vol. 73.

†77. Yorkshire Diaries and Autobiographies. Vol. II. Edited by C. Jackson and Margerison. See vol. 65.

†78. Memorials of Ripon. Vol. II. Edited by the Rev. J. T. Fowler. See vol. 74.

†79. Testamenta Eboracensis. Vol. V. Edited by the Rev. J. Raine. See vols. 4, 30, 45, 53, 106.

†80. The Life and Correspondence of the Rev. William Stukeley. Vol. III. Edited by the Rev. W. C. Lukis. See vol. 73.

†81. Memorials of Ripon. Vol. III. Edited by the Rev. J. T. Fowler. See vol. 74.

†82. A Selection from the Halmote Court Rolls of the Prior and Convent of Durham. Edited by W. H. D. Longstaffe and J. Booth.

†83. The Chartulary of Rievaulx. Edited by the Rev. J. C. Atkinson.

†84. Durham Churchwardens' Accompts. Edited by the Rev. J. Barmby.

†85. A Volume of English Miscellanies. Edited by the Rev. J. Raine.

†86. The Guisborough Chartulary. Vol. I. Edited by W. Brown.

†87. The Life of St. Cuthbert in English Verse. Edited by the Rev. J. T. Fowler.

†88. Three Northumberland Assize Rolls. Edited by W. Page.

†89. The Guisborough Chartulary. Vol. II. Edited by W. Brown. See vol. 86.

†90. The Brinkburn Chartulary. Edited by W. Page.

†91. The Yorkshire Chantry Surveys. Vol. I. Edited by W. Page.

†92. The Yorkshire Chantry Surveys. Vol. II. Edited by W. Page. See vol. 91.

†93. The Records of the Company of Merchant Adventurers of Newcastle upon Tyne. Vol. I. Edited by J. R. Boyle and F. W. Dendy. See vol. 101.

†94. Yorkshire Feet of Fines during the reign of King John. Edited by W. Brown.

†95. Memorial of St. Giles's, Durham, being Grassmen's Accounts, etc., together with documents relating to the Hospitals of Kepier and St. Mary Magdalene. Edited by the Rev. Barmby.

†96. Register of the Freemen of the City of York. Vol. I. Edited by F. Collins. See vol. 102.

†97. Inventories of Church Goods for the counties of York, Durham and Northumberland. Edited by W. Page.

†98. Beverley Chapter Act Book. Vol. I. Edited by A. F. Leach. See vol. 108.

†99. Durham Account Rolls. Vol. I. Edited by the Rev. J. T. Fowler.

†100. Durham Account Rolls. Vol. II. Edited by the Rev. J. T. Fowler.

†101. The Records of the Company of Merchant Adventurers of Newcastle upon Tyne. Vol. II. Edited by F. W. Dendy. See vol. 93.

†102. Register of the Freemen of the City of York. Vol. II. Edited by F. Collins. See vol. 96.

†103. Durham Account Rolls. Vol. III. Edited by the Rev. J. T. Fowler. See vol. 99.

†104. Knaresborough Wills. Vol. I. Edited by F. Collins.

†105. Records of the Newcastle Hostmen's Company. Edited by F. W. Dendy.

†106. Testamenta Eboracensia. Vol. VI. Edited by J. W. Clay. See vols. 4, 30, 45, 53, 79.

††107. The Rites of Durham. Edited by the Rev. J. T. Fowler. See vol. 15.

†† The price of this volume is £3.3.0.

in 1407 and 1423. Edited by K. C. Bayley, W. Brown and A. Hamilton Thompson. See vol. 37.

*128. The Registers of John le Romeyn, Archbishop of York, 1286-1296, Vol. II, and of Henry of Newark, Archbishop of York, 1298-1299. Edited by W. Brown. See vol. 123.

†129. Documents from the Records of the York Merchant Adventurers. Edited by Miss M. Sellers.

†130. Memorials of Fountains Abbey. Vol. III. Consisting of Bursar's Books, 1456-1459 and Memorandum Book of Thomas Swynton, 1416-1459. Edited by the Rev. J. T. Fowler. See vols. 42 and 67.

†131. A volume of 17th and 18th Century Northumbrian Documents. Edited by J. C. Hodgson.

*132. Horae Eboracenses. Edited by C. Wordsworth.

*133. Visitations of the North. Vol. II. Edited by F. W. Dendy. See vol. 122.

†134. The Percy Bailiff's Rolls at Alnwick Castle. Edited by J. C. Hodgson.

†135. Durham Protestations in 1641-1642. Edited by H. M. Wood.

†136. Liber Vitae Dunelmensis. Vol. I. Edited by A. Hamilton Thompson. See vol. 13.

†137. Early Newcastle Deeds. Edited by A. M. Oliver.

*138. The Register of Thomas Corbridge, Archbishop of York, 1300-1340. Vol. I. Edited by W. Brown.

†139. Fasti Dunelmenses. Edited by the Rev. D. S. Boutflower.

†140. Rituale Ecclesiae Dunelmensis. Edited by U. Lindelöf. See vol. 10.

†141. The Register of Thomas Corbridge. Vol. II. Edited by W. Brown and A. Hamilton Thompson. See vol. 138.

r142. Wills and Inventories from the Registry at Durham. Vol. IV. Edited by H. M. Wood. See vols. 2, 38, 112.

*143. The Statutes of the Church Cathedral of Durham. Edited by A. Hamilton Thompson.

*144. Visitations of the North. Vol. III. Edited by C. H. Hunter Blair. See vol. 122.

*145. The Register of William Greenfield, Archbishop of York, 1306-1315. Vol. I. Edited by W. Brown and A. Hamilton Thompson. See vols. 149, 151, 152 and 153.

*146. Visitations of the North. Vol. IV. Edited by C. H. Hunter Blair. See vol. 122.

     1406-37. Vol. I. Edited by R. L. Storey. See vols. 166, 169, 170, 177.

*165. Letters of Spencer Cowper, Dean of Durham, 1746-1774. Edited by E. Hughes.

*166. The Register of Thomas Langley. Vol. II. Edited by R. L. Storey. See vols. 164, 169, 170, 177.

*167. The Lawbook of the Crowley Ironworks. Edited by M. W. Flinn.

*168. Naworth Castle Household Accounts, 1648-1660. Edited by C. R. Hudleston.

*169- The Register of Thomas Langley. Vols. III-IV. Edited by
170   R. L. Storey. See vols. 164, 169, 177.

†171. Diaries of James Losh. Vol. I. Edited by E. Hughes. See vol. 174.

†172. Clifford Letters of the 16th Century. Edited by A. G. Dickens.

*173. Registrations of Durham Recusant Estates, 1717-1778. Part I. Edited by C. R. Hudleston. See vol. 175.

†174. Diaries of James Losh. Vol II. Edited by E. Hughes. See vol. 171.

*175. Miscellanea III containing Registrations of Durham Recusant Estates, Part II. Edited by C. R. Hudleston; and Durham Entries on the Recusants' Roll, 1636-1637. Edited by Miss A. Forster. See vol. 173.

*176. Northumberland Petitions. Edited by C. M. Fraser.

*177. The Register of Thomas Langley. Vol. V. Edited by R. L. Storey. See vols. 164, 166, 169, 170.

*178. The Correspondence of Sir James Clavering. Edited by H. T. Dickinson.

*179. Durham Episcopal Charters, 1071-1152. Edited by H. S. Offler.

*180.

LIST OF OFFICERS AND MEMBERS 1968

Patron and President

The Very Reverend J. H. S. Wild

Vice-Presidents

Sir Charles T. Clay (1925)
A. I. Doyle, (1958)
J. E. Fagg, (1958)
Miss C. M. Fraser (1966)
The Right Hon. Viscount Gort, M.C. (1939)
The Rev. Professor S. L. Greenslade (1945)
Mrs. N. K. M. Gurney (1966)
C. R. Hudleston (1956)
B. C. Jones, (1966)
Professor H. S. Offler (1966)
B. S. L. Surtees Raine, (1933)
Professor W. R. Ward (1966)

Secretary

W. A. L. Seaman,
County Record Office, County Hall, Durham

Editor

C. R. Hudleston,
28A Church Street, Durham

Treasurer

F. Stone,
Barclays Bank, Durham

iv

MEMBERS

(* denotes a Member of Council or Officer of the Society)

Addy, J., Esq., 60 Long Lane, Clayton West, Huddersfield
Baird, H. L., Esq., 1379 Garfield Place, Elizabeth, New Jersey, U.S.A.
Baker, L. G. D., Esq., Department of History, The University, Edinburgh
Barnes, E. R., Esq., 46 Woodside, Barnard Castle, Co. Durham
Benedikz B. S., Esq., New University of Ulster, Coleraine, Co. Londonderry, Northern Ireland
Birley, Professor Eric, M.B.E., The Old Fulling Mill, The Banks, Durham
Bond, M. F., Esq., Windyridge, Bolton Crescent, Windsor
Brockesby, R. Esq., The Elms, North Eastern Road, Thorne, Doncaster
Brown, Miss Margaret H., Ainthorpe, 78 Topcliffe Road, Thirsk
Cashman, Mrs. M. S., 4 Derwent Road, Cullercoats, Northumberland
Chaplin, S., Esq., 11 Kimberley Gardens, Newcastle upon Tyne 2
Clairville, Charles F., Esq., 208 Newman Street, Metuchen, New Jersey, U.S.A.
Clark, H, H., Esq., Aldham House, Barmoor Lane, Ryton, Co. Durham
Clark, Mrs. H. H., Aldham House, Barmoor Lane, Ryton, Co. Durham
*Clay, Sir Charles T., 30 Queen's Gate Gardens, London, S.W.7
Cliffe, B. P., Esq., Upholland College, Wigan
Cobham, The Venerable J. O., Archdeacon of Durham, The College, Durham
Corbitt, J. H., Esq., 73 Western Way, Darras Hall, Ponteland, Newcastle upon Tyne
Cowe, F. M., Esq., 2 Love Lane, Berwick-on-Tweed
Lord Crewe's Trustees, The Chapter Office, The College, Durham
Crosby, Mrs. J., 209 Gilesgate, Durham
Dickinson, H. T., Esq., 66 Montpelier Park, Bruntsfield, Edinburgh 10

Dodds, Miss M. Hope, Home House, Kells Lane, Gateshead 9

*Doyle, Dr. A. I., University College, Durham

English, J. G., Esq., Hazeldene, Husthwaite, York

*Fagg, J. E., Esq., The Prior's Kitchen, The College, Durham

Fenwick, J. T. F., Esq., Fenwick Ltd., Northumberland Street, Newcastle upon Tyne 1

Forster, Miss Annie, Burradon, Thropton, Morpeth, Northumberland

*Fraser, Miss C. M., Northbrook, King Edward Road, Tynemouth

Gibson, Sir W. W., Kingsmead, Riding Mill, Northumberland

*Gort, The Rt. Hon. Viscount, M.C., Hamsterley Hall, Rowlands Gill

*Greenslade, The Rev. Professor S. L., Christ Church, Oxford

*Gurney, Mrs. N. K. M., The Borthwick Institute of Historical Research, St. Anthony's Hall, York

Harrison, B. J. D., Esq., 17 Whitby Avenue, Guisborough

Harriss, G. L., Esq., Dean Court House, Eynsham Road, Botley, Oxford

Heesom, A. J., Esq., Department of History, 43-45 North Bailey, Durham

*Hudleston, C. R. Esq., 28a Church Street, Durham

Hughes, J., Esq., 12 Criffel Road, Belle Vue, Carlisle

James M. E., Esq., 30 Church Street, Durham

*Jones, B. C., Esq., The Record Office, The Castle, Carlisle

Leake, L. A., Esq., 22 St. John's Road, Neville's Cross, Durham

Lilburn, A. J., Esq., Newlyn, Abeyne, Aberdeenshire

Linker, R. W., Esq., 625 S. Pugh Street, State College, Pennsylvania 16801, U.S.A.

Loades, D. M., Esq., St. Mary's College, Durham

Malden, Rev. R. J., The Vicarage, Corbridge

Manders, F. W. D., Esq., 58 Longacre, Dairy Lane Estate, Houghton-le-Spring

Matthew, D. J. A., Esq., University College, Durham

McDermid, Rev. R. T. W., St. Mary's Vicarage, Cragside Walk, Leeds 5

McDonald, T. H., Esq., History Department, North Dakota State University, Fargo, North Dakota 58102, U.S.A.

Morimoto, Naomi, Esq., College of Economics, Nagoya Gakuin University, 10-7 Daiko-cho, Nigashi-ku, Nagoya City, Japan

Mosse, Rev. C. H., Canberra, 40 Oathall Road, Haywards Heath

Norris, R. C., Esq., Van Mildert College, Durham

*Offler, Professor H. S., 28 Old Elvet, Durham

Ollard, C. J. Esq., Scallows Hall, Binbrooke, Lincolnshire

Pearson, P. Chilton, Esq., 164 Campden Hill Road, London, W.8

Pease, R. A., Esq., Prior House, Richmond, Yorks.

Ramsay, The Right Reverend I. T., Lord Bishop of Durham, Auckland Castle, Bishop Auckland, Co. Durham

Reid, Mrs. J. C., 15 Lily Crescent, Newcastle upon Tyne 2

Rooksby, R. L., Esq., Department of Anthropology, University of Western Australia, Nedlands Western Australia 6009.

Rowland, T. H., Esq., Ridley House, 4 De Merley Road, Morpeth

Salvin, Capt. G. M., Croxdale Hall, Durham

Scarbrough, The Right Honourable the Earl of, Sandbeck Park, Rotherham

*Seaman, W. A. L., Esq., County Record Office, County Hall, Durham

Sheraton, Rev. B. R., 1 Moston Terrace, Edinburgh 9

Stewart, A., Esq., 9 Keswick Avenue, Sunderland

*Stone, Frank, Esq., Barclays Bank Ltd., Durham

*Surtees Raine, B. S. L., Esq., West Edleston, Gainford, Darlington

Tomlins, Col. L., Branksome Dene, 19 Queen's Road, Cheltenham

Tuck, J. A., Esq., Department of History, University of Lancaster, Bailrigg, Lancaster

Walker, R. F., Esq., 114 Runnymede Road, Ponteland, Newcastle upon Tyne

*Ward, Professor W. R., 5 Springfield Park, Durham

Warde-Aldam, Col. J. R. P., Frockley Hall, Doncaster

Webster, Mrs. E. M., O.B.E., Unthank Hall, Haltwhistle, Northumberland

Welford, M., Esq., 72 Station Road, St. Helen's Auckland

Wheeler, Miss E., Gladwynne, The Avenue, Coxhoe, Ferryhill

*Wild, The Very Reverend J. H. S., Dean of Durham, The Deanery, Durham

Woodward, F. H., Esq., The Manor House, Whitwell on the Hill, York

Woolstenholme, The Rev. C. E., St. Andrew's Vicarage, Spennymoor

Yasumoto, Minoru, Esq., 2-5-14 Higashi-Magome, Otaku, Tokyo, Japan

LIBRARIES AND INSTITUTIONS

Aberdeen, The University Library
Aberystwyth, The National Library of Wales
    The University College of Wales
Albany, New York, U.S.A., New York State Library
Ampleforth Abbey, Malton, Yorkshire
Ann Arbor, Michigan, U.S.A., The University of Michigan
    Library
Arlington, Texas, U.S.A., Arlington State College Library
Atlanta, Georgia, U.S.A., Emory University Library
Athens, Georgia 30601, U.S.A., The University of Georgia Libraries
Austin, Texas, U.S.A., The University of Texas Library

Baltimore, Maryland, U.S.A., Johns Hopkins University Library
    The Enoch Pratt Free Library
Barnard Castle, The Bowes Museum
Barnsley, The Public Library
Barrow-in-Furness, The Public Library
Belfast, The Queen's University Library
Berkeley, California, U.S.A., The General Library of the University
    of California
Bethlehem, Pennsylvania, U.S.A., Lehigh University Library
Beverley, The Public Library
Birmingham, The Public Library
    The Oratory Library, Oratory of St. Philip Neri, Edgbaston
    The University Library
Bolton, The Public Library
Boston, Mass., U.S.A., Boston Athenaeum
    Boston Public Library
    The New England Historical and Genealogical Society
Bradford, The Public Library
Bristol, The Public Library
    The University Library
Buffalo, New York, U.S.A., The Grosvenor Library

Cambridge, Trinity College Library
    The University Library

Cambridge, Mass., U.S.A., Harvard University Library
Canberra, The National Library of Australia
Canterbury, The Dean and Chapter Library
Carbondale, Illinois, U.S.A., Library of the University of Southern
    Illinois
Cardiff, The Public Library
Carlisle, The Public Library
Chester, The Dean and Chapter Library
Chicago, Illinois, U.S.A., The Newberry Library
    The University of Chicago Library
Cincinnati, Ohio, U.S.A., The Public Library
Cleveland, Ohio, U.S.A., The Public Library
Clinton, New York, U.S.A., Hamilton College Library
Columbia, Missouri, U.S.A., The University of Missouri Library
Copenhagen, Det Kongelige Bibliotek, (The Royal Library)

Darlington, The Edward Pease Public Library
Davis, California, U.S.A., University of California Library
Detroit, Michigan, U.S.A., The Public Library
Dewsbury, The Public Library
Downside Abbey, Stratton-on-the-Fosse, nr. Bath
Dublin, The National Library of Ireland
    The Library of Trinity College
Dundee, The University Library
Durham, Bede College
    The Dean and Chapter Library
    County Record Office
    Durham School
    St. Chad's College
    The University Library

Edinburgh, The National Library of Scotland
    The Public Library
    The University Library
Edmonton, Canada, The Rutherford Library of the University of
    Alberta
Evanston, Illinois, U.S.A., Northwestern University Library
    Seabury-Western Theological Seminary
Exeter, The City Library
    'The Roborough Library', The University of Exeter

Fargo, North Dakota 58102, U.S.A., The North Dakota State
University Library

Gateshead, The Central Public Library
Glasgow, The Mitchell Library
The University Library
Gothenburg, Sweden, The University Library
Guelph, Ontario, Canada, The University Library

Hanover, New Hampshire, U.S.A., The Baker Library,
Dartmouth College
Harrogate, The Public Library
Hartford, Connecticut, U.S.A., The Watkinson Library
Hartlepool, The Public Library
Haverford, Pennsylvania, U.S.A., Haverford College Library
Huddersfield, The Public Library
Hull, The Central Public Library
The University Library

Iowa City, U.S.A. The State University of Iowa Library
Ithaca, New York, U.S.A., Cornell University Library

Kansas, U.S.A., The University Library
Knoxville, Tennessee, U.S.A., The University of Tennessee Library

Leeds, The Central Public Library
The Leeds Library
The Thoresby Society
Trinity and All Saints Colleges
The University Library
The Yorkshire Archaeological Society
Leicester, The University Library
Lexington, Kentucky, U.S.A., The University of Kentucky Library
Lincoln, The Dean and Chapter Library
The Foster Library
Lincoln, Nebraska, U.S.A., University of Nebraska Library
Liverpool, The Public Library
The University Library
London, The British Museum
The City of Westminster Public Library
The College of Arms

The Goldsmiths' College Library
The Guildhall Library
The Inner Temple Library
The Institute of Historical Research
Lambeth Palace Library
The Law Society
The Library of the House of Lords
The Library of the London School of Economics
The London Library
The National Central Library
The Public Record Office
The Royal Historical Society
Sion College Library
The Society of Antiquaries of London
The Society of Genealogists
University College Library
Dr. Williams' Library
The University Library
London, Ontario, Canada, Huron College Library
Los Angeles, California, U.S.A., The Public Library
     The Library of the University of California at Los Angeles
Louvain, Belgium, Bibliothèque de l'Université
Lund, Sweden, Universitetsbibliotek

Madison, Wisconsin, U.S.A., The University of Wisconsin Library
Manchester, Chetham's Library
     John Rylands Library
     The Public Library
     The University Library
Melbourne, Australia, The Public Library of Victoria
Middlesbrough, The Public Library
Middletown, Connecticut, U.S.A., The Wesleyan University
     Library
Minneapolis, Minnesota, U.S.A., The University of Minnesota
     Library
Mirfield, Yorkshire, The House of the Resurrection
Missoula, Montana, U.S.A., The Library of the University of
     Montana
Montreal, McGill University Library
Morpeth, Northumberland County Library

Morgantown, West Virginia, U.S.A., West Virginia University
 Library

Nashville, Tennessee, U.S.A., Joint University Libraries
New Brunswick, New Jersey, U.S.A., Rutgers State University
 Library
Newcastle upon Tyne, The Central Public Library
        The Literary and Philosophical Society
        Northumberland County Record Office
        St. Dominic's Priory
        St. Mary's College
        The Society of Antiquaries of Newcastle upon Tyne
        The University, Department of Adult Education
        The University Library
New Haven, Connecticut, U.S.A., Yale University Library
New York City, U.S.A., Brooklyn Public Library
        Columbia University Library
        The General Theological Seminary
        New York Public Library
        The Union Theological Seminary
        The University of New York
New York, Binghampton, U.S.A., State University of New York
Northallerton, The North Riding County Council
Nottingham, The Public Library
        The University Library
North Shields, The Public Library

Oslo, Universitetsbiblioteket
Ottawa, Canada, Carleton University Library
Oxford, The Bodleian Library
        The Library of All Souls College
        The Library of Balliol College
        The Library of Corpus Christi College
        The Library of Exeter College
        The Library of Magdalen College
        The Library of the Queen's College
        The Library of St. John's College
        The Union Society

Paris, Bibliothèque Nationale

Philadelphia, Pennsylvania, U.S.A., The Biddle Law Library of
the University of Pennsylvania
The Free Library of Philadelphia
The University of Pennsylvania Library
Poughkeepsie, New York, U.S.A., Vasser College Library
Preston, Dr. Shepherd's Library
Princeton, New Jersey, U.S.A., Princeton University Library
Providence, Rhode Island, U.S.A., Brown University Library

Ramsgate, The Library of St. Augustine's Abbey
Reading, The University Library
Richmond, Virginia, U.S.A., Virginia State Library
Ripon, The Dean and Chapter Library
Rochester, New York, U.S.A., The University of Rochester Library
Rome, Biblioteca Apostolica Vaticana

St. Andrews, The University Library
Salt Lake City, Utah, U.S.A., The Genealogical Society of Utah
San Diego, Lajolia, California, U.S.A., University of California
Library
San Marino, California, U.S.A., The Henry E. Huntington Library
Sheffield, The Central City Library
The University Library
South Shields, The Public Library
Stanford, California, U.S.A., Stanford University Libraries
Stockton-on-Tees, The Public Library
Stonyhurst, Blackburn, St. John's College Library
Sunderland, The Central Public Library
Swansea, University College Library
Sydney, New South Wales, Australia, The Public Library

Thoresby Society, Claremont, 23 Clarendon Road, Leeds 2
Toronto, Canada, College of St. George Reference Library
The University of Toronto Library

University Park, Pennsylvania, U.S.A., Library of State University
of Pennsylvania
Uppsala, Sweden, Universitetsbibliotek
Urbana, Illinois, U.S.A., University of Illinois Library
Ushaw, Co. Durham, St. Cuthbert's College Library

Vancouver, Canada, University of British Columbia

Wakefield, West Riding County Library
Washington, D.C., U.S.A., The Library of Congress
Whitby, The Literary and Philosophical Society
Woolhampton, Berkshire, The Abbey of Our Lady and
    St. Edmund
Winston-Salem, North Carolina, U.S.A., Wake Forest College
    Library

York, The Borthwick Institute of Historical Research
    The City Public Library
    The Dean and Chapter Library
    York Philosophical Society
    York University Library
    The Yorkshire Architectural Society and the York
        Archaeological Society

During the Surtees Society's existence of 133 years it has produced 180 volumes, and is still endeavouring to fulfil the objects laid down by its founders. Although much has been accomplished, much remains to be done and there is still a wealth of material to be printed. The establishment of record offices in Cumberland, Durham, Northumberland, Westmorland and Yorkshire, has made many documents available to scholars for the first time. The Council of the Surtees Society, in conformity with the aims laid down in 1834, would wish to print many of these records. Printing costs have, however, risen so steeply of late years that the Society's present income is becoming inadequate for its needs. New members are urgently needed if the Society's work is not to be curtailed. Over the years the Society's volumes have helped scholars in all parts of the world, and we appeal to all who are interested in the Society's work to become members now, and help to maintain the high standards of the past. The annual subscription is £2 2s. a year, and applications for membership should be addressed to Dr. W. A. L. Seaman, County Record office, County Hall, Durham.

Future publications will include:

The Register of Thomas Langley, Bishop of Durham 1406-1437
sixth and concluding volume, with index to vols I—VI
edited by Dr. R. L. Storey

The Memorials of Archbishop Tobie Mathew
edited by Mr. Bernard Barr

Records of the Shipwrights' Company of Newcastle upon Tyne
sorted by Mr. H. T. Rowe

The York Memorandum Book
vol III edited by Mrs. Joyce Percy

Receipts

	£	s	d	£	s
SUBSCRIPTIONS—1968	271	16	7		
Arrears collected	34	0	10		
Paid in advance	21	0	0	326	17
SALE OF VOLUMES				749	3
INTEREST					
5% Defence Bonds	25	0	0		
5½% National Development Bonds	55	0	0		
Bank Deposit	76	4	9		
				156	4
				1,232	6
BALANCE AT BANK 1st JAN. 1968				2,048	5
				3,280	11

STATEMENT OF AFFAIRS

Liabilities

	£	s
SUBSCRIPTIONS PAID IN ADVANCE	21	0
CAPITAL ACCOUNT	5,636	4
	5,657	4

Payments

	£	s	d	£	s	d
ORTHUMBERLAND PRESS						
Vol. 178	767	1	6			
Vol. 179	690	1	6			
				1,457	3	0
MINISTRATION						
Postage	8	18	10			
Stationery	4	2	2			
Editor's expenses	14	18	1			
Clerical Assistance	30	0	0			
				57	19	1
SURANCE OF VOLUMES				8	1	0
				1,523	3	1
LANCE AT BANK 31st DECEMBER 1968				1,757	8	4
				3,280	11	5

AT 31st DECEMBER 1968

Assets

	£	£	s	d
VESTMENTS				
5% Defence Bonds	500			
5½% Nat. Development Bonds	1,000	1,500	0	0
OCK OF VOLUMES		2,317	10	0
EDITOR FOR VOLUMES SOLD		82	6	3
LANCE AT BANK		1,757	8	4
		5,657	4	7